A SAGE ON THE STAGE

COMMON-SENSE REFLECTIONS ON TEACHING AND LEARNING

MICHAEL ZWAAGSTRA

First published 2020

by John Catt Educational Ltd,
11 Plaza Real South, Suite 318,
Boca Raton, Florida 33432

Tel: 561.448.1987
Email: enquiries@johncatt.com
Website: www.johncatt.com

ISBN: 978 912906 70 3

Set and designed by John Catt Educational Limited

PRAISE FOR
A SAGE ON THE STAGE

"Education is less well than many people think. In particular, it's heavy with quack science, junk theory, snake oil, fads, tradition, dogma, and all manner of magic beans. But in the past few years we've started to see thinkers and writers and educationalists push back against the tidal wave of sloppy thinking. And spearheading this has been Michael Zwaagstra, whose cogent, concise, and clear thought pieces are exactly what the doctor ordered. I recommend his work, which cuts through the rubbish with reason and wit, to anyone interested in dragging teaching into the 21st century."

Tom Bennett, director of researchED
and author of *Teacher Proof*

"This collection of op-ed pieces provides a sobering, evidence-informed reflection on many popular, yet deeply flawed trends in education. Written by an active classroom educator, this book is a must-read for educators, parents, and others interested in sorting the wheat from the chaff in current education discourse."

Daniel Ansari, professor of psychology and
education, Western University, Ontario

"What a rarity. Sage advice from Michael Zwaagstra, a front-line secondary school teacher well equipped to cut through the education myths and cloud of edu-babble. At last, his pithy, probing, and no-nonsense commentaries can be found all in one place."

Paul W. Bennett, EdD, director of Schoolhouse Institute, Halifax, and founding program chair at researchED Canada

"Michael Zwaagstra deserves credit for presenting a clear, wide-ranging synopsis of many contentious educational issues. This easy read explains every fad and its deleterious impact on our education system. Michael's myth-buster is a valuable resource for skeptical educators, confused parents, and overly zealous politicians wanting to appeal for voter support by jumping on ill-conceived bandwagons."

Jim Dueck, EdD, author and retired assistant deputy minister at Alberta Education

"In this ordered collection of his op-eds, Michael presents a voice of realistic thought and reason in the wild jungle of educational fads, hypes, and eduquacks. A must-read for teachers, but more importantly for policymakers and politicians."

Prof. Dr. Paul A. Kirschner, dr.h.c., professor emeritus at the Open University of the Netherlands

CONTENTS

ACKNOWLEDGMENTS

THIS BOOK WOULD not have been possible without the ongoing support of my wife, Angela. Writing a book is a huge commitment and she willingly allowed me the time I needed to get it done. Any writer with a family knows the sacrifices that others must make in order for a book to be completed.

I am also grateful to the Atlantic Institute for Market Studies (aims.ca) and the Frontier Centre for Public Policy (fcpp.org), both based in Canada, for sponsoring my education research over the years. Most of the articles that appear in this book were originally published by one or both of these think tanks. This gave my education writing much greater exposure than it would have had otherwise.

Dr. Rodney Clifton and Dr. John Long have been mentors to me for many years. I studied under them as a university student and they have remained an ongoing source of support to me in my work. In addition, Dr. Clifton painstakingly edited most of my articles before they were first published. His sharp editorial eye has made my writing much better.

In recent years I have been inspired by the researchED movement (researched.org.uk), which was started in the

UK by the teacher Tom Bennett and brought to Canada by Paul W. Bennett (no relation). The conferences this group has organized have made research intelligible to classroom teachers and to the general public. Teachers, specifically, have been empowered to stand up against many of the useless fads being foisted on them. It is truly inspiring to see teachers around the world gather together to learn from each other about evidence-informed teaching practices.

I have been inspired by these colleagues and they stimulated some of the essays in this book. But any errors are mine alone.

DEDICATION

To Saphira and Jaydan

INTRODUCTION

SCHOOLS MAY RISE and fall, but education fads remain forever. Little did I know when I became a teacher that so much of my time would be spent fighting long-debunked fads that never seemed to go away.

It was in my university education courses that I first heard the absurd notion that a teacher should be a guide on the side rather than a sage on the stage. I was also taught that standardized testing was a poor way of assessing student achievement. Education professors told me that teachers didn't really need to be knowledgeable in the subjects they taught, since the most authentic learning experiences took place when teachers learned new things together with their students. I also heard all about individual learning styles, multiple intelligences, and many other half-baked theories that are popular in education faculties but rejected virtually everywhere else.

I pushed back against many of these ideas when I was a student, but it was a losing battle at the time. I quickly learned that a lowly student was no match for professors who had clearly spent their entire careers supporting and promoting these bad ideas. I also came to realize that if I wanted to get my degree, I had little choice but to go along with what my professors told me. So, I sucked it up and persevered through the nonsense.

Things got better when I finished university and began my career as a teacher. Finally, I was able to work with real students and leave some of the worst ideas behind me. However, I soon realized that useless fads extended far beyond the walls of education faculties. The more I read in education policy, the more I came to realize that many of the most common fads had little empirical evidence supporting them. This frustrated me and I resolved to do something about it.

In 2010, I co-authored *What's Wrong With Our Schools and How We Can Fix Them* with two like-minded education professors, Dr. Rodney Clifton and Dr. John Long. Our goal in writing that book was to draw attention to some of the most common problems in schools and to assist frustrated teachers and parents to fight back. The book got a lot of media attention and I heard from many teachers, parents, and other concerned citizens who appreciated the work we were doing.

After the publication of *What's Wrong With Our Schools*, I received invitations to speak to many groups. I also started writing articles on education policy. Most of these were written for the Frontier Centre for Public

Policy and the Atlantic Institute for Market Studies and appeared in major newspapers across Canada, including national newspapers such as *The Globe and Mail* and the *National Post*. The significant interest generated by these articles showed there was a strong desire for a common-sense approach to educational policy.

This book is a collection of my best educational articles over the past decade. As you will see by the titles, I've covered a lot of topics – everything from school discipline to content knowledge to no-zero policies. The articles are categorized into ten themes and, with the exception of minor edits, they appear as they were originally written. While many of the provincial governments mentioned in these articles have long since been replaced, readers will quickly see that the education issues remain relevant today. Governments may rise and fall, but education fads remain forever.

My hope is that this book will be of help to teachers, parents, school administrators, and school trustees in North America who are looking for a little less ideology and a whole lot more common sense in schools.

COMMON SENSE

~1~

FOOLISH EDUCATION FADS

GEORGE WASHINGTON, AMERICA'S first president, died in 1799 at the age of 67. A few days before his death, Washington spent several hours outside in the snow and sleet and refused to change his wet clothes. He developed severe chest congestion and had difficulty breathing. Given the seriousness of Washington's condition, his family summoned his doctors. It would been better if they had not.

The most common medical treatment in the 18th century, and for many centuries before, was bloodletting – the withdrawal of blood from a patient. Doctors thought this procedure helped to bring bodily fluids back into balance, by removing diseased blood. Unfortunately, it did nothing of the sort. In fact, bloodletting hastened death, since the last thing someone in a weakened medical state needs is to lose a vast quantity of blood. Had the doctors not removed five pints of Washington's blood, he might have survived his influenza.

It wasn't until the 20th century that bloodletting was finally abandoned as a standard first-line treatment. Medical research proved not only that bloodletting was harmful, but also that many more effective treatments were available. As research continued, doctors discovered increasingly better treatments and even some cures for the most devastating illnesses. In medicine, standard practice dictates that once a treatment is debunked, doctors stop using it. Thus, any doctor today who relied on bloodletting as a standard treatment would rightly face a malpractice lawsuit and no doubt lose their medical license.

If only things worked this way in education. Like medicine, education has seen its fair share of harmful practices foisted on unsuspecting teachers and students. Unlike medicine, however, these harmful practices continue long after they have been thoroughly debunked by research scientists. In other words, education continues to rely on fads – fads that are really education's own form of bloodletting. These practices are fads because they usually arise suddenly, lack any significant supporting evidence, typically fail, and then reappear under a new name. And so the cycle continues.

Some fads, such as individual learning styles, have gained widespread public acceptance, while others, such as a call to reduce the amount of "adultism" in schools, prompt widespread ridicule and mockery. Meanwhile, other fads, such as getting students as young as seven to specialize in a particular subject, are misapplications of legitimate scientific concepts. In this chapter's first article, you will see what this kind of misapplication looks like in practice.

One of the reasons we trust doctors is because they receive rigorous training in medical school and during their internships and residencies, where they learn to distinguish between effective and ineffective treatments. Sadly, the same isn't true for teachers. In fact, education schools are some of the worst purveyors of fads in the universities. As you will see in this chapter, education schools have long been held in low esteem by other university departments precisely because of their slavish devotion to fads. When education professors give presentations about the supposedly oppressive nature of dodgeball, they rightly open themselves up to ridicule by other professors and by parents.

Just as the doctors of today no longer rely on bloodletting, modern-day teachers should be set free from foolish fads. As you read these articles, you will likely be amazed at the staying power of the many fads in education.

SPECIALIZING IN EDUCATIONAL NONSENSE

AN ELEMENTARY SCHOOL in Alberta is taking the concept of specialization to a completely new level. At R. J. Hawkey Elementary School, students heading into Grade 2 will be expected to select a "major" that defines the focus of their education for the next three years.

These majors include the arts, sports, scientific inquiry, and humanitarian/environment. Teachers are required to tailor the provincial curriculum to match these specialty areas. Thus, students in the humanitarian/environment stream can expect to spend a lot of time in math calculating average recycling rates, while sports-stream students pore over team statistics.

The problem with this approach is that it inevitably leads to a further erosion of academic standards. While it may sound exciting at first for students to have their personal interests reflected in every school subject throughout the day, the novelty quickly wears off and reality sets in.

In order for students to become proficient in basic academic skills such as reading, writing, and mathematics, they need to spend time focusing specifically on these skills. Allowing students some flexibility in the books they read in class is one thing. Gearing their entire learning experience around a single theme is another. It is difficult to picture how this can be done without watering down academic standards.

The school claims to be inspired by Malcolm Gladwell's book *Outliers* (2008), which points out that 10,000 hours of practice are needed in order to achieve full mastery of a particular skill. However, the type of practice described by Gladwell is completely different from what this school is doing.

Gladwell notes that practice is concentrated in a focused area – a sport like hockey, or a musical instrument such as the violin. But calculating the velocity of a hockey puck in math class won't count towards the 10,000 hours of practice that a prospective NHL player needs. Nor will reading yet another short story about the Amazon rainforest move students any closer to some special proficiency level in ecology.

The four specializations arbitrarily chosen by this school appear to have more to do with indoctrinating students in politically correct ideology than promoting academic excellence. The reality is that many, if not most, students learn best in a school environment where they receive focused academic instruction in the core academic subjects. In other words, let science be science and math be math. Students can learn these subjects without having their every fancy and whim catered to by a school system more focused on self-esteem than academic excellence.

One of the purposes of school is to expose children to new ideas and expand their horizons. Students have plenty of time outside of school hours to explore hobbies and other areas of personal interest. In addition, there are many ways in which teachers can, and do, help students to pursue their interests that don't involve restructuring their entire elementary education.

An important life lesson is that we don't always get to do what we want. Even people working in professions that they love acknowledge that some days their jobs are not very exciting. But they still come to work the next day because that's how the real world works.

Some might look at what is happening in R. J. Hawkey School and ask whether this is similar to the school-choice model provided by Canadian school boards such as Edmonton. The answer is that the two are nothing alike. R. J. Hawkey School is forcing all students to choose one of four specializations, whether they like it or not. In contrast, parents in Edmonton are free to enrol their children in the schools of their choice, including those that follow a traditional model of education. Furthermore, Edmonton students regularly take literacy and numeracy proficiency tests and all schools, including specialized schools, are expected to show academic progress.

There is a big difference between giving parents the option of enrolling their children in the school of their choice and forcing all seven-year-old students in one school to choose a so-called "major" that becomes the focus of all their subjects. Schools should spend less time trying to be at the cutting edge of every education fad and more time looking at ways to raise academic standards.

This article was originally published in 2010

REAL BRAIN-BASED LEARNING

MANY EDUCATION GURUS are renowned for promoting theories that have limited empirical support. One of the best examples is the work of "brain-based education" guru Eric Jensen. His promotional website proudly proclaims his specialty to be the "integration of cutting-edge neuroscience with practical, user-friendly brain-based learning classroom strategies." That's a rather bold statement for someone who, until receiving a PhD in human development in 2014, had only a BA in English and no public school teaching experience.

Like many other education gurus, Jensen downplays the importance of factual knowledge and academic content, and makes clear that he is not a fan of requiring students to do a lot of rote memorization. Fortunately, there are some people with real cognitive expertise who are challenging the misguided approach of armchair neuroscientists like Jensen.

Daniel Willingham, a psychology professor at the University of Virginia, has written an informative book for educators called *Why Don't Students Like School?*. Willingham, who has a PhD in cognitive psychology from Harvard University, is an expert in how the human mind works. In his book, he uses several widely accepted principles of cognitive psychology to make his case for more traditional methods of instruction.

For example, Willingham notes that there is good reason for requiring students to practice their multiplication tables and memorize the spelling of commonly used words. This is because lack of space in working memory is the key bottleneck in human cognition. In other words, students who do not know their math facts by heart find it very difficult to perform more advanced problems, since they end up wasting valuable mental capacity on something that should be automatic.

Although education gurus often deride repetitive practice as "drill and kill," the fact is that it provides the foundation for deeper learning. We do our brains a significant favour when we commit basic skills to memory, because it frees up our working memory for other things. It may not be very exciting to practice doing the same thing over and over, but it pays off in the long-term.

Willingham also dissects the claim by education gurus that schools need to spend less time teaching students about science and history and more time helping them to think like scientists and historians. These gurus argue that reading about scientific discoveries in a textbook or hearing a lecture about major historical events are far removed from the work that scientists and historians actually do. As a result, they propose that schools should decrease the amount of emphasis placed on the acquisition of factual knowledge.

However, Willingham points out that this advice is hopelessly misguided. Scientists and historians became experts in their field through many years of study and practice. Students need to have a broad-based understanding of the academic basics before they can even begin to think like experts. It is impossible to think deeply about something you know little about. After all, it would be foolish to expect a detailed historical analysis of the root causes of World War I from a student who didn't know, by memory, the names of the major countries involved in that conflict.

In addition, since students with the broadest knowledge base are the ones best able to make sense of the world around them, schools should focus on giving them solid academic content from as young an age as possible. Education gurus do our students a grave disservice when they minimize the importance of content.

Willingham also effectively debunks the multiple-intelligences theory of the educational psychologist Howard Gardner. According to Gardner, traditional IQ tests are not an accurate measure of intelligence since they do not measure other so-called intelligences, such as musical ability and interpersonal skills. But while it is true that students have many different talents and skills, most cognitive psychologists reject the way in which Gardner redefines the very nature of intelligence. In fact, there is little empirical data supporting the sweeping claims that he makes.

It is ironic that the theory of multiple intelligences is widely rejected by psychological experts, yet enthusiastically embraced within the school system. One can only hope that educators pay more attention to where the evidence really points.

Everyone who wants to know what real brain-based learning looks like should take the time to read Willingham's book. It certainly exposes the flaws in the progressive ideology promoted by many education gurus.

PERSONS OF CANADA MUST FIGHT BACK AGAINST THE THOUGHT POLICE

LADIES AND GENTLEMEN, it's time we call a spade a spade. English-speaking Canadians must learn to speak inclusively. Whether you are a long-time resident or a recent immigrant, choose your words more carefully. After all, we should make sure that Christians, Jews, Muslims, Hindus, Buddhists, and atheists all feel equally included in our society. Inclusivity begins at home when mothers and fathers model appropriate language for their kids.

Gratefully, I'm not an employee of the Durham District School Board in Ontario. If I were, what I just wrote could get me in serious trouble with their language police. In fact, I violated their Guidelines for Inclusive Language more than a dozen times in my first paragraph. That could be enough to classify me as a level-one cultural destroyer on their cultural proficiency continuum.

You see, their guidelines prominently display a chart with six different levels. They range from level one, cultural destructiveness, to level six, cultural proficiency. Being tolerant doesn't count for much in this school district – it only gets you up to level two and is also called cultural incapacity. To reach the highest level of inclusiveness and attain cultural proficiency, you need to master a whole new lingo.

For starters, beginning a speech with the phrase "ladies and gentlemen" is verboten. Apparently, audiences are supposed to be addressed with a more neutral greeting, such as "men and women." Similarly, you should not refer to people as husbands or wives – they are all simply spouses. Teachers are also expected to replace the terms mother and father with the more neutral title of "parent or guardian."

According to the guidelines, the idiom "calling a spade a spade" can't be used since it allegedly "demean[s] and ostracize[s] people." Apparently, bigots in the US sometimes used the word "spade" as an ethnic slur against African Americans during the early 20th century. So, notwithstanding that this English phrase dates back to 1542 and ironically means to tell the truth in a direct way, it still can't be uttered by Canadian teachers.

The silliness doesn't stop there. It is now officially wrong to refer to someone as Chinese, Korean, or even American. Instead, teachers should identify someone as a person from a particular country. So, calling Barack Obama an American is a no-no. Rather, we should say that he is a person from America. When the country music artist Lee Greenwood sings that he is "proud to be an American," we should change that to "proud to be a person from America."

By the way, the same applies to faith and language groups. No longer can teachers identify someone as Jewish, Muslim or Christian. Rather, they should be identified as members of a particular faith community. For example, the American evangelist Billy Graham was not a Christian, he was a person from the Christian community. By the same token, we cannot refer to someone as English-speaking or French-speaking, but instead as a person who speaks a particular language.

Let's put this into practice and see how it works in real life.

François Legault is a person from Quebec, a person who speaks French, and a member of the Roman Catholic community. Unfortunately, some of his comments during the 2018 Quebec election campaign could be interpreted as hostile to immigrants.

Oops, I did it again. I used a level-one cultural destroyer phrase when I said the word immigrants. According to the Durham District School Board, I'm supposed to refer to them as newcomers instead. Someone should really tell the minister of immigration, I mean the minister of newcomers, that he insults millions of new Canadians, sorry, persons from Canada, whenever he calls them immigrants.

Isn't it great to know that the Durham District School Board values diversity? In fact, it is so committed to diversity that it has issued a document that forces everyone to speak in exactly the same way.

If we want to see real improvement in our schools, perhaps administrators should spend more time focusing on academic achievement and no time creating politically correct language guidelines for students and staff. All persons from Canada should be outraged at this silliness going on in our schools.

FAILED EDUCATION FADS SHOULD BE BURIED, NOT RESURRECTED

THE 1970S WAS a memorable decade. Judging by yearbook pictures from that era, everyone wore polyester, bell bottoms, platform shoes, and long hair. This may be a fun way to dress up at Halloween costume parties, but virtually everyone recognizes that fashions from the past belong in the past.

And while poor fashion choices from the seventies have mercifully been retired, the same cannot be said of failed education fads. In fact, open-area classrooms, one of the worst fads from that era, are making a comeback in schools across North America.

The theory behind open-area classrooms is relatively simple: schools should have as few walls as possible in order to facilitate collaboration among teachers and students. By making school designs open, students are exposed to learning all around them. The buzz of learning permeates the school as students eagerly construct new knowledge and work together to build a collaborative professional learning community.

However, things didn't quite work out that way in real life. Open-area classrooms proved to be an unmitigated disaster. They were too noisy and distracting. Teachers and students alike found it impossible to function effectively in an environment that prevented them from getting some peace and quiet. By the 1980s, most open-area schools were retrofitted with classroom walls and the failed experiment seemed to come to an end.

It seems that in the field of education, however, fads never actually die out. Rather, they disappear for a while and reappear later under new names. When they do, school administrators jump on the "new" idea and seek to impose it on as many schools as possible. As more schools adopt the latest fad, it gains the appearance of inevitability. Eventually, after it acquires near-total dominance, the fad comes crashing down as everyone realizes it doesn't work. It then lies low or dormant, until it is once again reinvented and foisted on an unsuspecting new generation of students and teachers.

The reappearance of open-area classrooms under the new label of open-concept schools is the latest example. Fielding Nair International, an architecture firm that specializes in this approach, has designed more than 400 schools around the world, along with approximately a dozen in Western Canada. About half of those schools are located in Regina, where the public school board appears to have put all its eggs in the open-concept basket.

In 2012, Douglas Park Elementary School opened with great fanfare in suburban Regina. As proof of its fidelity to an open-concept layout, this school has huge open spaces, lots of windows, and movable walls. During the opening ceremonies, the school's principal praised the random abstract layout of the building as "innovative." The director of education at Regina Public Schools dutifully added that the new school was not merely a building, but rather a "community of learners." If only the guests had thought to bring their bell bottoms and platform shoes, the trip back to the seventies would have been complete.

It's remarkable that any school board would invest so heavily in an approach that lacks supporting evidence. When Prakash Nair of Fielding Nair International makes grandiose claims about classrooms being obsolete in the 21st century, many educators rightly view his work with skepticism.

Nair's design has ideological motivations. As he himself acknowledges in his writings, his advocacy of open-concept schools is closely linked to his belief in the constructivist approach to teaching. Constructivism holds that, instead of passing on a defined body of knowledge, teachers should help students to construct their own understanding of the world around them. Open-concept schools go hand-in-hand with this approach. Interestingly, whole language and the "new math" are examples of two other failed fads that stem from constructivism. There are good reasons to be skeptical of any approach based on constructivism, considering its dismal track record.

To cap it all off, there is no empirical research establishing that open-concept schools lead to improved student achievement. However, there is a lot of evidence that students and teachers alike find it difficult to function when their learning environment is noisy and filled with distractions.

Far from being on the cutting edge of innovation, open-concept schools merely recycle a failed fad from the past. School boards should leave this concept in the seventies, where it truly belongs.

EDU-BABBLERS SHOULD
STOP HORSING AROUND

DO YOU EVER read Berenstain Bears books with your kids or watch old Disney movies such as *Bambi* and *The Jungle Book?* Maybe you sing "Old MacDonald had a farm" or "Five little monkeys jumping on the bed" when goofing around with them.

If you do, you might be poisoning their minds with "racist, colonial, consumerist, heteronormative, and patriarchal norms." At least, that's the concern raised by Nora Timmerman and Julia Ostertag in their paper "Too Many Monkeys Jumping in Their Heads: Animal Lessons Within Young Children's Media." It was published in the *Canadian Journal of Environmental Education* and formally presented in 2013 at the Congress of the Humanities and Social Sciences in Victoria, British Columbia.

In their paper, Timmerman and Ostertag argue that popular children's stories about animals promote anthropocentrism – the belief that humans are the most important species on the planet. Apparently, when children see cartoon animals dressed up like humans and walking on their hind legs, they get sucked into the idea that humans are superior to animals. This can lead to "feelings of angst and disconnection," "the loss of community," and even "extensive animal extinction."

I never realized that letting my kids read Garfield comics would have such a negative impact on the future of the planet. Ironically, the real cats in our house right now do seem an awful lot like Garfield, in that they eat and sleep a lot. But then again, our cats are domestic pets and I get the feeling Timmerman and Ostertag don't approve of that either.

Timmerman and Ostertag are also critical of any movies and cartoons in which animals have human-like conversations. As a case in point, they describe an episode of *Sesame Street* in which Big Bird learns the value of acceptance during a conversation with a "real" bird. While they acknowledge that the lesson about acceptance is a good one, Timmerman and Ostertag wonder "where the actual birds' voices went." They go on to suggest that children's books should only portray animals speaking their natural languages.

Now that is an interesting idea. Clearly, the author of *Charlotte's Web* got it all wrong when he portrayed Charlotte as a clever, talking spider and Wilbur as a lonely but thoughtful pig. Instead, the author should have written a story in which a pig simply rolled in the mud and said "oink, oink" while the spider above him captured and ate bugs. I'm sure that would have been a real hit with kids!

Some of the issues raised by Timmerman and Ostertag are downright silly. For example, they ask, "When we jump on the bed and sing 'five little monkeys jumping on the bed,' does it teach children that they are connected to monkeys through a similar wild spirit, or does it teach them that monkeys are careless and accident prone?" Maybe it isn't intended to teach anything at all and is just a fun little rhyme parents like to repeat when their kids are jumping on the bed.

After hearing about this article, you might wonder what academic discipline actually accepts such politically correct nonsense as genuine scholarship. The fact that both Timmerman and Ostertag were PhD students in the faculty of education at the University of British Columbia should answer that question. Only in an education course could it be considered serious scholarship to write a paper in which you explain how uncomfortable you are with how animals are portrayed in children's books.

Perhaps education professors should spend less time worrying about the impact of cartoon animals on children and more time dealing with the real challenges facing our schools.

THERE IS NO SUCH THING AS INDIVIDUAL LEARNING STYLES

ONE OF THE most widely accepted "truisms" in public education is that all students have individual learning styles. As a result, teachers are expected to tailor their lessons to meet the needs of the visual, auditory, and tactile-kinesthetic learners in their classes.

For example, suppose a Grade 3 teacher wants to introduce her students to the solar system. According to learning styles theory, visual learners should be shown lots of pictures of the planets, while auditory learners benefit more from a detailed verbal description. Meanwhile, tactile-kinesthetic learners should construct models of each planet. In this way, each student learns about the solar system through his or her individual learning style.

The theory sounds so simple and elegant. Many books and articles have been written showing teachers how to adapt their lessons to meet the learning styles of each student. However, there is just one little problem. Learning styles are a myth.

In his book *When Can You Trust the Experts?* (2012), the cognitive psychologist Daniel Willingham explains how to test learning styles theory. Take a group of people and identify each person's so-called learning style. Let half of them experience a story through their preferred learning style – for example, the story could be conveyed by pictures to visual learners and recited verbally to auditory learners. Then make the other half experience the same story through a different learning style. If the theory is correct, people who experience the story through their preferred learning style should remember it better than those who do not.

"Experiments like this have been conducted," writes Willingham, "and there is no support for the learning styles idea. Not for visual, auditory, or kinesthetic learners, nor for linear or holistic learners, nor for any of the other learners described by learning styles theories." In other words, learning styles theory is no more valid than an urban myth.

Willingham is not the only expert to point this out. John Hattie, director of the Melbourne Education Research Institute at the University of Melbourne, has reviewed thousands of studies about student achievement in the course of his research. In his book *Visible Learning for Teachers* (2012), Hattie bluntly states that there is "zero supporting evidence" for learning styles.

Catherine Scott, an Australian education researcher who has closely examined the evidence for learning styles theory, came to the same conclusion. Her article "The Search for the Key for Individualised Instruction" appeared in the *International Guide to Student Achievement* (2013) and concluded that any activities based on learning styles theory "represent a waste of precious teaching and learning time."

Despite the lack of evidence for individual learning styles, the theory remains widely promoted by provincial education departments, faculties of education, and public school boards. For example, *Rethinking Classroom Assessment with Purpose in Mind*, a document published in Canada in 2006 by Manitoba Education, stresses the importance of identifying the individual learning styles of each student. A more recent Manitoba Education document, *Strengthening Partnerships*, recommends that teacher candidates be placed in a classroom environment where "teaching practices incorporate an understanding of different learning styles."

The damage caused by this failed theory is significant. Instead of providing well-designed whole-class lessons, teachers often waste vast amounts of time trying to adapt to the so-called learning styles of each student. Then, at their professional development in-services, these same teachers are pushed to go even further in this direction. As a result, they end up working harder, getting worse results, and burning themselves out in the process.

Rejecting the theory does not mean teachers should teach every topic in exactly the same way. It makes sense to use a variety of strategies when introducing students to new concepts. Going back to our example of Grade 3 students learning about the solar system, a good teacher will do far more than simply give a single lecture. Rather, she will show her students pictures of the planets, provide accurate verbal descriptions, and give students an opportunity to work with models of the planets.

Good teachers have always used a host of strategies to engage as many students as possible. Sometimes looking at a picture is the best way to get a concept across, while at other times it makes sense to let students construct a model. There is no need to pigeonhole students into different learning styles, particularly since there is no evidence that such styles exist. Individual learning styles are a myth that should finally be put to rest.

NOTHING NEW UNDER THE SUN WITH EDUCATION FADS

"THE THING THAT hath been, it is that which shall be; and that which is done is that which shall be done: and there is no new thing under the sun" (Ecclesiastes 1:9 KJV).

King Solomon may have written these words nearly 3000 years ago, but I can't help but wonder whether he had the endless cycle of education fads in mind. A new fad is introduced with great fanfare, pushed on teachers, falls out of favour when it proves to be a flop, and then, a generation later, is renamed and foisted on a whole new group of unsuspecting educators.

That is certainly what came to my mind in early 2016 when CBC Radio profiled a new US documentary called *Most Likely to Succeed*. Basically, the premise of this documentary is that the current school system, with its distinct subject areas and defined period lengths, is based on an outdated 19th-century factory model and schools need to shift to a more project-oriented approach that encourages creativity and collaboration among students and teachers.

To get a rundown on this movie, CBC interviewed Matt Henderson. At the time, Henderson was a social studies teacher at St. John's-Ravenscourt School in Winnipeg, and he had run for the New Democratic Party in the 2015 federal election; now he is an assistant superintendent in Winnipeg. Henderson gave the film a glowing review and noted that it featured High Tech High, a San Diego charter school that put many of the film's ideas into practice.

Interestingly, the moment Henderson mentioned that High Tech High was a charter school, he felt the need to explain that, unlike charter schools in Canada, charter schools in the US are 100% publicly funded. However, Henderson's statement is wrong. The only Canadian province where charter schools exist is Alberta and all charter schools in that province are 100% publicly funded, just like in the US. Needless to say, Henderson's factual blunder at the beginning of the interview did not sit well with me.

As for the ideas promoted in the film itself, Henderson explained that High Tech High and other project-based schools have done away with bells, and instead of distinct subject areas such as history, chemistry, and physics, the schools are built around "educative experiences." Teachers from different subject areas collaborate on designing projects that are built around the interest of students. It all sounded very exciting and revolutionary.

However, the truth is that there is nothing new about any of this. In 1918, William Heard Kilpatrick, a well-known American education professor, wrote an article for *Teachers College Record* entitled "The Project Method" in which he outlined the exact same approach. He suggested that the school day should be centred around projects of interest to students (such as kite-building) since these are "purposeful acts in the educative process." Had Kilpatrick not already published his article in 1918, I might have assumed he had plagiarized Henderson's CBC comments.

Nearly 20 years later, Kilpatrick made his radical views even more explicit in his book *Remaking the Curriculum* (1936). In it, he blasted the traditional separation of subjects as an "older outlook" that is "the antithetical opposite of the best available conceptions both of the life process and of learning." In true progressive fashion, Kilpatrick even made sure to explain that the process of learning is far more important than any specific factual content.

Teachers like Henderson may buy into the myth that *Most Likely to Succeed* is a cutting-edge film promoting a revolutionary approach to learning for the 21st century.

The reality is that it merely repackages and recycles the very old ideas of Kilpatrick. When it comes to education fads, there really is nothing new under the sun.

EDUCATION FADS DO KIDS
AND TEACHERS NO FAVOURS

STUDENT ACHIEVEMENT IS declining in Nova Scotia. The 2014–15 accountability report from the province's Department of Education makes this abundantly clear.

Barely half of Grade 8 students are meeting expectations in math, while the writing skills of students in grades 3 and 6 have declined by nearly 20 points in two years. Nova Scotia students also score below the Canadian average in national and international assessments.

Surprisingly, the education minister, Karen Casey, is doubling down on cosmetic reforms. As a case in point, the minister plans to bring in provincial teaching standards, in partnership with the Nova Scotia Teachers Union (NSTU). But these standards are unlikely to do anything other than create more paperwork for teachers and administrators.

Because of the union's involvement in creating the standards, it is certain that ironclad teacher tenure provisions will remain in place. There is no way the union is going to agree to anything that could potentially make it easier for school boards to fire ineffective teachers.

Instead, teachers will likely spend more time filling out questionnaires, creating useless portfolios, and implementing the latest meaningless education fads. They may even get more coaching in how to write edu-babble on report cards or attend professional development sessions featuring assessment gurus who promote no-zero policies or other nonsense. One thing Casey's new teaching standards will not do is improve student achievement.

Here's a novel idea for Casey: stop pushing education fads on teachers and just let them teach. Teachers don't need provincial guidelines for writing report card comments, nor do they need to waste their time learning how to use the latest technological gadgets in their classrooms. They also don't need onerous assessment rules that make it nearly impossible to hold students accountable for late or incomplete work.

Unfortunately, the union has been complicit in the promotion of such useless fads. In recent years, the NSTU has twice brought in the American education speaker Alfie Kohn to indoctrinate elementary teachers in the latest progressive education fads. Some of Kohn's more radical ideas include the abolition of all grades for students, the removal of virtually all direct instruction, and prohibiting teachers from praising students when they do something good or correcting them when they get an answer wrong. These harebrained ideas are not what teachers need to hear at their professional development sessions.

If we really want to improve student achievement, the people who run our education system need to cut out the edu-babble and focus on what actually works. Mike Schmoker, a former teacher and administrator, makes this abundantly clear in his book *Focus: Elevating the*

Essentials to Radically Improve Student Learning (2011). In Schmoker's view, schools should focus on three simple things: a reasonably coherent curriculum, sound lessons, and purposeful reading and writing in every discipline. Get these right and student learning will improve. It's that simple!

When it comes to classroom instruction, the last thing students need is more flashy hands-on activities and "project-based learning." Innovation is no guarantee of student learning. In fact, lessons can be quite effective with a minimal amount of technology, so long as the teacher sets specific learning objectives, provides direct instruction focused on those objectives, and regularly checks for student understanding.

A big part of the problem is that school boards, education departments, and teachers' unions keep bringing in professional development consultants who promote the same failed fads. From Kohn's anti-grading ideology to Marian Small's fuzzy math to Ken O'Connor's no-zero approach to assessment, teachers are bombarded with a host of bad ideas. No wonder student achievement is suffering.

Instead, teachers deserve to know that research supports traditional methods such as direct instruction, and that there is nothing wrong with standing at the front of the classroom and showing the whole class the correct way to solve a problem. Similarly, there are good reasons to make students memorize basic facts and practice basic skills until they become automatic. Content knowledge is far from outdated in the 21st century.

Casey may think that imposing a new set of standards on teachers is going to improve student achievement. However, these standards will only be useful if they promote what actually works in the classroom. Meaningless education fads have got to go.

This article was originally published in 2016

A CHILDISH OBSESSION WITH ADULTISM

LIKE MOST PEOPLE, I believe there are significant differences between adults and children, particularly when it comes to maturity levels. These differences explain why voting is restricted to adults, why children cannot purchase alcohol or cigarettes, and why all children are required to attend school. There are good reasons why children do not have the same rights as adults.

However, to some politically correct activists, this common-sense principle is actually unjust discrimination. They even have a word for it: adultism.

Adam Fletcher is an educational consultant and speaker based in the US. He writes extensively about school reform and argues that schools need to do much more to empower students. He also believes that adultism is the main thing holding schools back.

In an article entitled "Adultism in Schools," Fletcher sets forth a sweeping definition of adultism. "Bias towards adults happens anytime the opinions, ideas, knowledge, beliefs, abilities, attitudes, or cultures of adults are held above those of people who aren't considered adults. Because of this, our very conception of schools is adultism at work," he explains.

Well, when you put it that way, our entire society is guilty of adultism. Apparently, it's discriminatory to believe that the opinions of adults have any more validity than those of children. When it comes to running a school, students should have just as much input as teachers and principals. Anything less than full equality is adultism.

Fletcher does not shrink from the logical implications of his quest to eliminate adultism. He contrasts "convenient" student voice with "inconvenient" student voice, and notes approvingly that the latter includes topics that impact teaching or governance of the school. Fletcher even complains about the fact that school boardrooms and school counselor offices are designed for adults rather than children.

Of course, old-fashioned people like me would probably argue that these rooms were built that way because only adults are school board trustees and school counselors. I might also point out that meeting rooms and offices are adult workspaces that need to be appropriately designed for professionals to do their work. But there I go again with my adultist bias.

Fletcher's crusade against adultism stems from his desire to transform schools into student-centred institutions. He believes that "adultism makes schools today ineffective." He even quotes the well-known education writers John Dewey and Paulo Freire, to show that his anti-adultist agenda fits logically with their progressive ideals.

However, while Dewey and Freire were strong proponents of student-centred learning, neither of them went nearly as far as Fletcher. Ironically, by quoting these two education writers, Fletcher is guilty of adultism himself, since he didn't quote any children to back up his position. Perhaps this has something to do with the fact that all education writers are adults.

Fletcher's ideas have met with widespread ridicule but, incredibly, they are being taken seriously in some schools across North America. His consultancy, SoundOut, provides teacher professional development in school divisions and Fletcher is a highly sought-after public speaker. His website is replete with endorsements from education professors, teachers, and school administrators.

It never ceases to amaze me how crackpot theories like Fletcher's opposition to "adultism" manage to infiltrate the school system. Giving students a moderate amount of input into how schools are run is one thing. Radically overhauling schools so that we don't favour adult voices in any way is another thing entirely.

EDUCATION FACULTIES FAIL TO PREPARE NEW TEACHERS TO BE EFFECTIVE

IN 1933, THE retiring president of Harvard University, Lawrence Lowell, famously stated that his university's school of education was "a kitten that ought to be drowned."

Of course, university presidents wouldn't talk like this today. But Lowell was far from the only scholar to hold education schools in such low repute – and for good reason. In 1954, *Time* magazine reflected the prevailing sentiment when it dubbed New York's 120th Street, which separated Columbia Teachers College from Columbia University, as "the widest street in the world."

Generally speaking, academics held education schools in low repute because these schools promoted progressive educational theories that de-emphasized traditional academic content. Nowhere was this more evident than at Columbia Teachers College, where John Dewey and his disciple William Heard Kilpatrick promoted a child-centred educational approach in which factual knowledge took a back seat to fads such as "project-based learning."

Fast-forward to 2019 and things haven't changed much. Education schools continue to downplay subject-specific knowledge and promote many of the same fads, albeit under new names. Today's education students are fed platitudes such as the need to be a guide on the side rather than a sage on the stage. And instead of empowering future teachers with the confidence they need to effectively manage their classrooms, education professors promote theories that have little practical use in actual classrooms with real students.

One of the most common sentiments expressed by classroom teachers is that they were taught little about how to teach. They give high praise to their teaching practicums, where they spend time in real classrooms, but quickly follow this up with a comment about how useless they found their education classes.

Imagine what would happen if other groups of professionals – such as lawyers, doctors or dentists – regularly expressed such disdain for their training programs. Governments would initiate a major review of these professional schools to find out the problem. However, because no one has the courage to step in and make major changes, education schools continue to offer mediocre – or worse – programs. Thus, the cycle continues.

There is a better way. While education schools often tilt from one useless fad to another, there is a defined body of research regarding which methods work best in the classroom. For example, research clearly shows that, when it comes to learning how to read, phonics is far superior to whole language. Dr. Jeanne Chall, former director of the Harvard Reading Laboratory, demonstrated the superiority of phonics in the 1960s. It's unfortunate that many education schools ignore the overwhelming evidence for phonics and continue to push whole-language methodologies on to student teachers.

Fortunately, some teachers are taking matters into their own hands. In 2013, the British teacher Tom Bennett organized the first researchED conference in London. This event generated so much teacher interest that it quickly became a worldwide phenomenon, with conferences in dozens of countries.

ResearchED is different from typical teacher professional development because it's entirely teacher-directed and provides an opportunity to directly engage with the research literature. In contrast to the ideological conformity expected at education schools, researchED presenters come from a variety of perspectives and disciplines, and teachers can make up their own minds regarding what they hear.

The Australian teacher Greg Ashman, who is pursuing a PhD in instructional design, is a regular researchED presenter. His book *The Truth About Teaching: An Evidence-Informed Guide for New Teachers*

(2018) is vastly superior to any textbook used in education schools. As a case in point, Ashman recognizes the value of whole-class instruction led by the teacher and provides useful strategies for classroom management.

Ashman also exposes teachers to cognitive load theory, something all teachers need to understand. Cognitive load theory notes that working memory is limited and that basic information must be transferred to long-term memory in order to free up space in the brain for more complex problems. This is why the memorization of math facts, such as the times tables, is very important. Committing these facts to memory makes it possible for students to tackle more advanced math concepts. It's unfortunate that prospective teachers typically learn next to nothing about cognitive load theory in education schools.

If education schools want a better reputation, they need to become less ideological and more evidence-focused. This would reduce the vast gulf between them and other university departments. But for now, that gulf is still "the widest street" on campus.

FAULTY EDUCATION THEORIES OPPRESS DISADVANTAGED STUDENTS

IS DODGEBALL A harmless game or legalized bullying? This was the riveting topic of a paper presented by three education professors at the Canadian Society for the Study of Education's 2019 annual conference.

Shortly after the *National Post* published a story about this presentation, media outlets across the country picked it up and the debate went viral. The three co-presenters – Joy Butler of the University of British Columbia, Claire Robson of Simon Fraser University, and David Burns of Kwantlen Polytechnic University – appeared on multiple radio and TV stations defending their critique of dodgeball, often in the face of incredulous interviewers.

Much of the debate revolved around dodgeball itself. Many fans were dismayed at how their sport was attacked by educational theorists. The head of Dodgeball Canada, in fact, penned an opinion piece for the *National Post* defending dodgeball as "built on the foundation of teamwork, inclusiveness, and trust." Meanwhile, the *Toronto Star* columnist Emma Teitel took a contrary view in a column entitled "Maybe getting rid of dodgeball isn't such a bad idea." Clearly, the battle lines have been drawn.

However, focusing on the merits and demerits of dodgeball as a sport misses the point, because it overlooks the authors' thesis.

According to the conference website, Butler, Robson, and Burns examined dodgeball through "the ethic of anti-oppressive education" and concluded that "the hidden curriculum of dodgeball reinforces the five faces of oppression." In other words, the authors used a particular ethical framework to examine dodgeball as a game. This means the validity of their conclusions depends on the reasonableness of their framework.

The abstract of the paper notes that Iris Marion Young's book *Justice and the Politics of Difference* (1990) provided the theoretical basis for the authors' understanding of the five faces of oppression: exploitation, marginalization, powerlessness, cultural domination, and violence. In many ways, Young's emphasis on group identity was a precursor to today's identity politics, where a person's membership, or lack of membership, in a marginalized group takes precedence when evaluating ideas.

By tying their critique of a children's game, dodgeball, to Young's radical theory, Butler, Robson, and Burns set dodgeball up to fall short on ethics, since no competitive sport could emerge unscathed under this theory. Instead of asking whether dodgeball is a healthy activity for children to enjoy, the authors focused on whether marginalized students were picked last for teams and if other students targeted them while playing the game. Obviously, this critical approach assumes that bullying behaviour is caused by the game of dodgeball rather than being an unfortunate, yet common, reality of childhood.

In contemporary identity politics, phrases such as "check your privilege" accuse entire groups of benefiting unfairly from their race and/or gender, even when this isn't true of all individuals within the group. As a case in point, the Canadian prime minister, Justin Trudeau, may be a privileged white male, but an unemployed fisherman in rural Newfoundland is probably not.

Accusing well-meaning people of being oppressors solely because of their membership within a group is hardly conducive to productive dialogue. In fact, it is prejudice, because it attributes the general characteristics of the group to the individual when there is considerable variability between individuals even within the group.

Interestingly, even the admission policies of many education faculties reflect an obsession with group identity. For example, the University of Manitoba's faculty of education reserves nearly half its spaces for students from five diversity categories: Indigenous, racialized, LGBTQ, persons with disabilities, and disadvantaged. This sends the unfortunate message that membership in one (or more) of these groups trumps the qualifications and merit of the individual.

Sadly, an obsession with group identity is now the norm rather than the exception within Canadian faculties of education. In their courses, prospective teachers often learn more about promoting social justice than about effective ways of teaching reading, science, and math. Even though there is a wealth of evidence backing up the importance of ensuring that students acquire subject-specific content knowledge through teacher-led instruction, education professors typically dismiss this in favour of trendy child-centred approaches.

This explains why education students typically spend so much time reading and discussing Paulo Freire's book *Pedagogy of the Oppressed* (1968). Like Young, Freire assumed that capitalist societies oppress minority and marginalized groups. Freire's critique of the so-called "banking model of education" advances his view that students should co-learn together with their teachers, rather than have knowledge transmitted to them by knowledgeable teachers.

The problem with this approach is that it hurts the students it intends to help. By de-emphasizing the importance of content knowledge, Freire's modern-day disciples make it nearly impossible for students from disadvantaged homes to close the knowledge gap between themselves and students from upper-class homes. One could even argue that education faculties are systematically oppressing disadvantaged students when they promote misguided theories about teaching and learning.

Stories about the oppressive nature of dodgeball may provide comic relief for readers, but this concern reflects a real problem with education faculties. Faulty education theories do a lot of harm to students, particularly those from disadvantaged homes.

MANDATORY E-LEARNING IS YET ANOTHER FAD

THOMAS EDISON IS considered one of the world's greatest inventors. Some of his inventions include the incandescent light bulb, the phonograph, and the motion picture camera. There is no doubt that Edison's ideas have made the world a better place.

However, Edison had even higher hopes for some of his inventions. In particular, he was convinced that the motion picture camera would transform education. In 1922, he boldly predicted: "I believe that the motion picture is designed to revolutionize our educational system and that in a few years it will supplant largely, if not entirely, the use of textbooks."

Obviously, things didn't turn out the way he expected. Although his motion picture camera found its way into classrooms, it did not transform learning. Textbooks are still used for serious teaching and learning. Clearly, Edison was better at inventing things than he was at predicting future trends in education.

Lest we become too critical of Edison, it's important to remember that he is far from the only person to think that a new piece of technology is going to transform learning. Similar claims have been made about everything from calculators to desktop computers to iPads. What's far less forgivable is the way in which governments and school boards ignore the lessons of history and continue putting so many resources in the technology basket.

In early 2019, Ontario's then education minister, Lisa Thompson, announced that all students in the province would be required from 2020 to complete four e-learning courses in order to graduate from high school. This announcement came out of nowhere. A handful of US states require students to finish one e-learning course, but no province or state requires students to complete four courses. In addition, no stakeholder groups, neither the unions nor the educational experts, had recommended this initiative. The minister seemed to have generated it on her own.

Online learning obviously has some benefits. Online courses tend to have flexible schedules and students can complete them at their own pace. In addition, students at smaller and isolated schools can often take required courses by distance. When used as a supplement to regular programming, e-learning is a great way to expand the options available to many students.

However, by mandating e-learning for every Ontario student, the provincial government has fallen into the trap of making technology, rather than learning, the focus. Of course, technology is a valuable tool – but it is only a tool. Since there is no evidence that students learn better through e-learning than through traditional classroom instruction, it doesn't make sense to make e-learning mandatory for all students. It would be like scrapping textbooks and forcing all teachers to show educational videos to their students.

The July 2019 cabinet shuffle, in which Stephen Lecce replaced Thompson as education minister, raised hopes that the government planned to roll back some of her most misguided initiatives. Unfortunately, Lecce has given no indication that he will budge on the mandatory e-learning courses. A recent statement from his office, emphasizing "the need to bring the education system into the 21st century by utilizing leading-edge technologies," suggests that the new education minister is doubling down on this initiative.

But a recent survey of more than 6000 students conducted by the Ontario Student Trustees' Association should give the government cause for concern. Not only did almost 95% of respondents say they "disapprove of the new e-learning mandate," but a significant number of those who had taken e-learning courses in the past faced major hurdles in completing them, from wi-fi problems and difficulty understanding the course content to not having a teacher available.

The vast majority of high school students oppose this change, and so do the vast majority of teachers and parents. It's one thing to ignore public opinion when there is strong research behind an initiative. It's another thing entirely to implement an untested initiative in the face of strong public opposition. Surely, this is a recipe for failure.

The reality is that most students already spend more than enough time looking at computer screens. Research is clear that when it comes to improving student achievement, the things that matter most include strong teacher-student relationships, direct instruction, coherent curriculum, focused practice, and timely feedback from teachers. These things take place in classrooms with teachers, not on computer screens in bedrooms.

It is ironic that the Ontario government has stated that it wants to move away from education fads, particularly in math instruction. Replacing a math curriculum focused on discovery learning with a content-rich curriculum that includes practice, memorization, and standard algorithms – that is the type of reform that schools need. In contrast, mandating e-learning courses has all the hallmarks of a fad. A very expensive one.

~2~

RAISING ACADEMIC STANDARDS

IN 1957, THE Soviet Union shocked the world when it launched the first satellite into orbit. The successful launch of Sputnik 1 shattered the confidence of Americans who had fully expected the US to win the space race. Shaken from their complacency, politicians and pundits sought to find out how their country could have lost this race. It didn't take long to point the finger at a culprit – the American education system.

Life magazine ran a series of articles bemoaning the low academic standards in American schools. Politicians responded quickly. In 1958, Congress passed the National Defense Education Act, while schools rushed to beef up their math and science course offerings. The push was on to substantially raise academic standards across the country.

This was far from the first or last time there was a public call to raise academic standards in schools. However, like many other political slogans, raising academic standards is easier said than done. What, exactly, does it mean to raise academic standards?

The first article in this chapter answers this question by pointing to the long-standing debate between progressive and traditional approaches to education, and makes a case for traditionalism. This is followed by an piece that further backs up this position with research. Other articles in this chapter tackle topics such as practice and memorization, along with the need for teachers to expose students to more than one perspective when dealing with controversial topics.

The final piece in this chapter makes the case for a stronger emphasis on Canadian history in curriculum guides. Although this article was initially geared toward teachers and parents in Canada, the arguments are equally applicable to teachers and parents in Britain and the US. American readers will be particularly interested to see that the push by many progressive educators to tear down statues erected in honour of controversial historical figures, such as General Robert E. Lee, is not limited to the US. Incredibly, a Canadian teachers' union has called for all buildings named after Canada's first prime minister, John A. Macdonald, to be renamed.

The only way we can have an informed discussion about buildings and statues is for the broader public to have a solid understanding of their country's history. Until we raise our academic standards, we should expect these important debates to continue generating more heat than light.

Raising academic standards isn't just about making students do more work, it's also about teaching more effectively so that students learn more. If we put mediocrity in, we can expect mediocrity out. But the education of our children is too important for us to tolerate mediocrity.

WHAT IS THE PURPOSE OF EDUCATION?

MOST PEOPLE AGREE that public schools play an important role in society. For example, virtually everyone agrees that students should become good citizens and have the necessary skills to succeed in the world.

After all, it's fairly obvious that we expect schools to prepare students for something. Otherwise, there wouldn't be much point in their spending 13 (or more!) years of their lives in school. If schools weren't important, it's unlikely that provincial governments would spend more money on education than almost anything else.

So, progressives and traditionalists both agree that we want our graduates to be well-educated. But what exactly does this mean?

As a traditionalist, I believe that schools exist primarily as instruments of cultural preservation and transmission. In other words, there is a specific body of knowledge with which all students must be familiar in order to function effectively in society. Reading, writing, and performing basic mathematics are timeless skills that will never become obsolete. As a result, it is imperative that schools ensure that our students master these skills. Furthermore, it is important for students to have an understanding of key scientific concepts and to be familiar with the history of their own country.

E. D. Hirsch, Jr., a well-known education reformer and former University of Virginia English professor, describes this knowledge base as cultural literacy, or core knowledge. Schools exist to ensure that students graduate with a common knowledge base and essential set of skills.

In other words, students should be able to pick up a newspaper and read it with understanding. This means that, in addition to deciphering the words, they should have enough background knowledge of the world around them to be able to understand what they read. If students have to visit Google or Wikipedia to look up the major concepts mentioned (such as parliamentary democracy, vaccinations, or the Middle East), schools have largely failed in their task.

Progressives often respond to this argument by noting that the vast increase in the amount of information available to us makes it impractical to identify a core knowledge base with which all students should be familiar. They claim that we need to teach students *how* to access information, rather than identifying *what* information they should receive.

This argument overlooks the fact that the information explosion makes it even more imperative for students to receive a common grounding in core skills and knowledge. Allowing students to learn only what they are personally interested in is a recipe for an even more fragmented society than we have today.

We should also keep in mind that no one who supports traditional education believes the curriculum should specify so much content for students that they have no time to learn anything else. Rather, there should be a balanced approach where at least half of what students learn is the same as what students in other schools are learning. The remaining time can be used to delve into issues of more personal interest to students.

If students are taught this core knowledge base effectively, they are, in essence, already learning how to acquire additional information. In fact, there is room for progressive approaches in classrooms so long as students still acquire the fundamental knowledge and skills that they need to succeed in the world.

In addition to helping students acquire a solid knowledge base, schools must also help them to develop self-discipline. By self-discipline I mean a willingness to take responsibility for your actions and put in the necessary time and effort to complete a task. Self-discipline also means that you don't allow setbacks to stop you from pressing onward.

Employers want and need employees who are reliable, punctual, respectful, and competent. An employee who lacks self-discipline will likely not remain employed for very long. Schools should serve as a training ground so that students who graduate are prepared for life in the real world.

The traditional model of education best fits the goal of ensuring that school graduates become good citizens. Good citizens understand the world they live in and choose to contribute to it in a positive way. In order for this to happen, graduates need to have a core knowledge base and the necessary self-discipline to function effectively in the workforce.

TRADITIONAL TEACHING METHODS SUPPORTED BY RESEARCH

IF THERE'S ONE thing drilled into the heads of prospective teachers, it is that traditional teaching approaches are hopelessly outdated. Our future educators are told that it is wrong to think of classrooms as places where students acquire knowledge from teachers.

Instead, prospective teachers are immersed in a philosophy known as constructivism. In essence, constructivism encourages students to construct their own understanding of the world around them, and reduces teachers to mere learning facilitators.

This philosophy finds its roots in the writings of the 18th-century French philosopher Jean-Jacques Rousseau, yet there are many modern proponents as well. Paulo Freire, a well-known educational theorist, criticized the "banking" theory of schooling in his classic book *Pedagogy of the Oppressed* (1968). Freire and his disciples saw education as an inherently political act of liberation, rather than the transmission of essential knowledge and skills to students.

This stands in stark contrast to the traditional view that schools exist for the purpose of ensuring that students acquire the necessary knowledge and skills to function effectively in society. Unfortunately, the constructivist approach disavows this belief and minimizes the importance of academic content.

It was this philosophy that inspired the replacement of phonics with the whole-language approach for reading instruction. Phonics reflects the traditional approach of teaching children letters and sounds, while whole language encourages children to construct their own meaning from what they read. Although most current reading programs incorporate aspects of phonics, significant components of whole language remain prevalent in elementary classrooms.

Constructivism has made its presence felt in other subject areas as well. Math teachers are often encouraged to do less direct instruction of specific number concepts and more real-life application of math principles. Some textbooks and curriculum materials even recommend that teachers turn their math classes into social justice indoctrination sessions.

One example of this is *Math That Matters (2006)* by David Stocker. This book, written by a Toronto educator, contains 50 suggested math lessons for teachers. The lessons address controversial topics from a decidedly left-wing perspective. Students learn to promote the union movement, challenge the dominance of evil corporations, and blame industrialized countries for the world's hunger problems.

It should come as little surprise that this propagandistic volume was published by the Canadian Centre for Policy Alternatives, a self-styled "progressive" think tank. *Math That Matters* forms part of the CCPA's education project, which was designed as a response to concerns about the influence of corporations over public education. The political inclination in this type of resource should be obvious.

Advocates of constructivism assert that research proves their methods are superior to more traditional approaches. However, a book written by John Hattie, director of the Melbourne Education Research Institute at the University of Melbourne, challenges this claim.

Visible Learning (2009) was born out of Hattie's 15-year synthesis of thousands of research studies into what makes the biggest difference to student achievement. He found that constructivist approaches did not produce the promised results. "The role of the constructivist teacher is claimed to be more of facilitation to provide opportunities for individual students to acquire knowledge and construct meaning through their own activities," writes Hattie. "These kinds of statements are almost directly opposite to the successful recipe for teaching and learning."

In contrast, traditional methods had a significant positive impact on student learning. As an example of this, Hattie found that phonics outperformed whole language by a huge margin. He concluded that phonics was "powerful in the process of learning to read," while the effects of whole language on reading instruction were "negligible."

One of the largest studies cited by Hattie was Project Follow Through, a long-term study involving more than 72,000 students over ten years. This study contrasted direct instruction (a traditional methodology) with constructivist approaches such as whole language and open education. Even though researchers found direct instruction was the only approach to have significant positive effects on student learning, the study simply led to more money being spent on failed constructivist approaches.

Hattie is right when he describes education as an immature profession that often places ideology ahead of evidence. Even though the actual research evidence supports traditional teaching methods, constructivist ideology remains dominant in teacher training institutions.

It's time for us to place evidence ahead of ideology and adopt teaching methods that actually enhance student learning.

SCHOOLS SHOULD FOCUS ON THE ESSENTIALS

WHEN EVERYTHING IS a priority, nothing is a priority. Nowhere does this expression hold more true than in our public schools.

The length of the school day may have remained essentially unchanged for the past few decades, but the same cannot be said about the expectations placed upon classroom teachers. In addition to providing academic instruction, a classroom teacher today is expected to perform the roles of social worker, nurse, police officer, and counselor, to name just a few. With all of these responsibilities, it's a wonder teachers have time to do any teaching at all.

Provincial governments don't make it any easier when they regularly expand the mandate of public schools into areas that go far beyond academic instruction. For example, the Manitoba government encourages schools to focus on social justice and environmental sustainability initiatives, while the Ontario government micromanages schools down to the level of banning unhealthy food from canteens. None of this has much, if anything, to do with the instructional mandate of schools.

Fortunately, some educators have begun pushing back against this trend. Mike Schmoker's book *Focus: Elevating the Essentials to Radically Improve Student Learning (2011)* shows how important it is for schools to focus on the essentials. As a former teacher and school administrator, Schmoker writes with the confidence of someone with firsthand experience in the field. In his view, schools need to focus on three simple things: a reasonably coherent curriculum, sound lessons, and purposeful reading and writing in every discipline. Any school without each of these three things in place should refuse to begin any new initiative until the situation is remedied.

Schmoker argues that curriculum documents are unnecessarily complex and often swamped in meaningless verbiage. In Canada, this is most apparent in English language arts (ELA), where thick curriculum guides contain almost nothing of substance. Trivial standards such as "find the main idea," "identify the proper sequence of events," and "distinguish between major and minor characters" do little to promote meaningful literacy. In fact, these guides are so generic and useless that high school teachers can faithfully teach the entire ELA curriculum without requiring students to read a single complete book or write a single formal essay.

According to Schmoker, a simplified ELA curriculum that identifies specific books and articles all students should read, and defines the number and length of formal papers to be written at each grade level, would go a long way toward improving academic standards. Curriculum standards should be based on academic content rather than meaningless edu-babble.

Schmoker notes that students are more likely to learn when teachers focus on providing effective whole-class lessons rather than trying to cater to the individual learning style of every student. He provides several examples of schools in high-poverty neighbourhoods where their students are reading well above grade level. In these schools, early years teachers engage all students in learning through whole-class lessons with regular checks for understanding.

The incorporation of purposeful reading and writing in every discipline is also recommended by Schmoker. He argues that many teachers are too quick to avoid the use of textbooks in classroom instruction. Reading dense, complex prose found in textbooks is an excellent way for students to improve their reading skills and acquire valuable content knowledge simultaneously. Students should also spend more time writing tightly focused essays in which they interact with books and articles. Schmoker asserts that essay writing is an excellent all-in-one assessment of a student's reading and writing abilities and should therefore be done regularly.

Schmoker is absolutely right when he notes that some things have a much bigger impact on student achievement than others. A coherent curriculum, sound lessons, and purposeful reading and writing activities are essential to improving the amount of student learning that takes place.

Instead of adding new initiatives and dumping more responsibilities on teachers, provincial politicians and school division administrators should follow Schmoker's advice and focus on what matters most. Students and teachers alike would benefit greatly from this approach.

MORE GRAMMAR AND LESS EDU-BABBLE PLEASE

IN 2013, A group of graduate students staged a sit-in during Professor Val Rust's class at the University of California, Los Angeles (UCLA). They did this to protest against an allegedly "toxic" racial climate in the Graduate School of Education and Information Studies.

What terrible thing happened in Rust's class that precipitated this drastic behaviour? Did he belittle minority students with racist epithets or openly defend white superiority? No, he didn't.

According to UCLA's newspaper, the *Daily Bruin*, some students didn't like the spelling and grammar corrections that Rust made on their dissertation proposals. During their demonstration, these students described Rust's corrections as "micro-aggressions."

However, in a letter sent to his colleagues, Rust explained his side of the story. "I have attempted to be rather thorough on the papers and am particularly concerned that they do a good job with their bibliographies and citations, and these students apparently don't feel that is appropriate," he wrote.

Rust's explanation sounds reasonable to most people outside of education schools. All university students, regardless of their racial background, need to use proper spelling and grammar. This is particularly true in graduate school, where students are pursuing master's and doctoral degrees. A student who cannot write properly is unlikely to experience much success in the academic world. One might think that graduate education students, most of whom have been teachers, would understand this requirement better than any other students.

However, it is no coincidence that this protest happened in an education school. Education schools have long been obsessed with issues of race and culture, to the detriment of the academic basics. I experienced this personally during an education graduate course. Throughout the course, the professor and students made repeated references to "white privilege" and frequently bashed Western civilization for being racist and sexist.

During one of our discussions, the professor even suggested that there was too much focus on reading and writing in public schools. In her opinion, reading and writing was only one form of literacy and other forms deserved equal attention. Many students backed up the professor's position. One of them went so far as to argue that the excessive focus on print-based literacy was an unfortunate example of the so-called neoliberal agenda.

Education professors at other universities have long expressed similar points of view. Several years ago, *The Globe and Mail* in Canada published a letter from Heather Lotherington, an education professor at York University in Toronto, arguing that "grammatical knowledge and mastery of spelling and punctuation" are the "literacies of a half century ago." But she didn't stop there. "Literacy now requires mastery over digital tools for collaborative, dynamic, multimodal communication. Continuing to test children's formal spelling using handwriting is a speck on the team-oriented strategizing and programming abilities they will need to succeed," she wrote.

For those who don't speak edu-babble, here's the rough translation: "Students don't need to learn how to spell because their computers have spell-check."

The good news is that many teachers reject this nonsense. In 2012, Jim McMurtry, a high school English teacher in British Columbia, wrote an article that appeared in the news magazine of the BC Teachers' Federation. In it, McMurtry bemoaned the removal of grammar from the provincial English curriculum. He noted that it was possible for students to "score a 100% on the English 12 exam with grammatical and spelling errors in their writing."

McMurtry also correctly pointed out that it was unrealistic to expect students to use proper grammar in their writing if they never learned the components of sentences or the proper use of punctuation marks. Each of these things needs to be directly taught, but most English curriculum guides pay only minimal, if any, attention to grammar and punctuation. As a result, students may never learn basic grammar skills.

The root of the problem is that education schools, and the professors who teach in them, have long been obsessed with things like social justice and racial perspective, and not basic knowledge and skills. Education schools have lost sight of what actually matters in the real world.

Students would benefit from less edu-babble and more spelling and grammar teaching in our schools. Contrary to what many education professors argue, basic knowledge and skills aren't obsolete.

MEMORIZATION, PRACTICE, AND CRITICAL THINKING GO HAND IN HAND

ALL STUDENTS SHOULD become critical thinkers. This goal is agreed upon by virtually all educators. The ability to synthesize and evaluate information, and come up with new ways of looking at things, is highly prized in education circles from kindergarten to graduate school. As it should be.

Given the importance of critical thinking, it's not surprising that schools across Canada and around the world proudly trumpet the progress they make in developing this skill. It's also increasingly common for provincial education departments to rave about "21st-century skills," one of which is critical thinking. Yet, in falling for the glitzy and overhyped promises of the 21st-century skills movement, they are discarding tools that are proven to work.

The reality is that if we want students to become critical thinkers, they need to memorize facts – lots of them. They also need to spend plenty of time doing rote learning – consolidating knowledge and skills through practice and repetition – so that the facts become embedded in their long-term memories. This is not the focus of the 21st-century skills movement, but it is supported by a wealth of research evidence.

John Hattie is director of the Melbourne Education Research Institute at the University of Melbourne and one of the world's foremost experts on educational research. His findings do not support the claim that critical thinking skills can be taught in isolation from content. Hattie makes this clear in a 2016 article for the journal *npj Science of Learning*. "These [21st-century] skills often are promoted as content free and are able to be developed in separate courses (e.g., critical thinking, resilience). Our model, however, suggests that such skills are likely to be best developed relative to some content. There is no need to develop learning strategy courses or teach the various strategies outside the context of the content," he writes.

The reason for Hattie's conclusion is simple: students cannot think critically about something they know nothing about. Surface learning, which includes the memorization of basic facts and vocabulary, is just as important as deep learning, since deep learning cannot take place in the absence of knowledge. Students need to acquire lots of knowledge, most of which needs to be taught directly by competent teachers.

Once surface knowledge has been acquired, students need to consolidate and transfer it to their long-term memories, so it can be retrieved automatically when they want to think critically. As Hattie explains, "Although some may not 'enjoy' this phase, it does involve a willingness to practice, to be curious and to explore again, and a willingness to tolerate ambiguity and uncertainty during this investment phase."

Critical thinking cannot be taught in isolation because it depends on content. For example, there is a huge difference between applying advanced mathematical principles and analyzing the factors that led to a major historical event. Both require critical thinking, but there is no reason to assume that students can do either of these things without first acquiring substantial background knowledge and then consolidating it through practice.

Proponents of 21st-century skills may think of critical thinking as an isolated skill that does not depend on specific content, but research from Hattie and many other psychologists shows otherwise. It is a huge mistake to downplay curriculum content and replace it with critical thinking strategies. If we want students to become critical thinkers, we need to make sure they acquire and consolidate as much surface knowledge as possible. Only then will deeper learning take place.

BALANCED LITERACY IS A POOR WAY TO TEACH READING

THE READING WARS should be over. Unfortunately, they are not.

In the late 1960s, Dr. Jeanne Chall, former director of the Harvard Reading Laboratory at Harvard University, compared the phonics and whole-language approaches to reading instruction. The evidence overwhelmingly showed that phonics was superior to whole language. Subsequent researchers came to the same conclusion.

This should have settled the matter, but whole-language advocates refused to admit defeat. That's because the emphasis placed by whole language on students choosing books of interest to them fits naturally with the child-centred philosophy espoused by progressive educators for more than 100 years. In contrast, phonics, with its emphasis on the systematic teaching of letter-sound correspondences, is widely associated with a more traditional approach.

However, despite the strong ideological commitment to whole language by many educators, it became increasingly difficult to hold on to this program. Whole language's many failings were widely reported in the media and it soon fell out of favour with the general public. Nevertheless, as happens with many failed education fads, advocates of the approach managed to rebrand it as something different. Enter balanced literacy.

Balanced literacy purports to combine the best of phonics and whole language. Students read books of interest to them and receive phonics instruction from teachers on an as-needed basis. Lucy Calkins, founding director of the Teachers College Reading and Writing Project at Columbia University in New York, is probably balanced literacy's best-known proponent. Since Calkins is also a whole-language supporter, it should come as no surprise that balanced literacy instruction looks a lot more like whole language than phonics.

In order for phonics to be effective, letter-sound correspondences must be taught in a systematic way. By relegating phonics to brief mini-lessons occurring only when students encounter problems with understanding specific words, balanced literacy deprives them of the focused phonics instruction they actually need. It's like a buffet chef loading up customers' plates with as much dessert as possible, while providing only tiny portions of nutritious food.

Balanced literacy has two unique features that distinguish it from both whole language and phonics: levelled books and reading comprehension instruction. Unfortunately, both of these make balanced literacy worse than its predecessors. Levelled books, which are common in balanced literacy classrooms, are assigned a letter, from A to Z, indicating their relative reading difficulty. Students are then expected to choose books from the level at which they are reading, regardless of the book's content.

However, reading levels fail to account for the important connection between specific content knowledge and reading comprehension. Research shows that students who know a lot about a particular topic can read almost any book about it, no matter its assigned reading level. Conversely, students who know little about a topic will struggle with books that are below their reading levels.

Perhaps the worst feature of balanced literacy is the way it reduces reading comprehension to a set of non-content-specific strategies. As a result, students spend hours engaging in pointless and mind-numbingly boring activities such as "identifying the main idea," "making inferences," and "recognizing story structure." The thinking behind this approach is that students will be able to use these strategies with any text, regardless of the topic.

However, the best predictor of reading comprehension is prior background knowledge about a topic, not the use of reading comprehension strategies. Someone who knows a lot about mid-19th-century Canada, for example, is far more likely to comprehend an article about George Brown's call for "rep by pop" for Canada West than someone who knows nothing about the topic.

In order to read and understand an article, students must be able to do two things. First, they need to know how to decode the individual words in the article; second, they need to comprehend, or make sense of, what they are reading. This is why thoughtful reading instruction is so important. Decoding is best taught through systematic phonics, while comprehension is primarily determined by the accumulation of background knowledge.

Unfortunately, balanced literacy gets both these things wrong. It relies primarily on the discredited whole-language approach for decoding words and it turns reading comprehension into a series of non-content-specific strategies. As a result, students are left floundering. In contrast, effective reading programs combine the direct and systematic teaching of phonics with a curriculum that is content-rich. In this type of instruction, students actually learn how to pronounce unfamiliar words and they can understand what they are reading. The material is both interesting and challenging.

Balanced literacy programs should be replaced with reading instruction that actually places an appropriate balance between phonics and knowledge acquisition. This would be the best way to bring an end to the reading wars.

TEACHERS MUST EXPOSE STUDENTS TO MORE THAN ONE PERSPECTIVE

THERE'S A FINE line between teaching and brainwashing. Teaching informs students about the world around them and helps them to become critical thinkers. In contrast, brainwashing provides students with heavily skewed information that leads to one predetermined conclusion. It's easy to mix these two things up if we aren't careful.

People who work in schools are called teachers rather than brainwashers for very good reason – there's a world of difference between teaching students what to think and teaching them how to think. Teachers should challenge students' thinking by exposing them to contrary ideas, as opposed to indoctrinating students with their world view.

Unfortunately, there's reason to believe that some teachers are blurring the line between teaching and brainwashing. For example, a Canadian public school teacher made the news in 2017 when he had his Grade 6 and 7 students work on a variety of climate change projects. The unit culminated in a public event where students made presentations about how to stop climate change.

Obviously, climate change is an important issue and it makes sense for students to learn about it. However, the teacher in question had spent time at an intensive training session led by the former US vice-president Al Gore. That teacher is now a "climate-reality leader" who is expected to train other teachers in how to take action on climate change. This probably explains why he had his students watch Gore's latest movie, *An Inconvenient Sequel*, during class.

This teacher went far beyond informing students about climate change. His climate change unit was designed to make his students take action that conformed to what he learned at the Gore training session. That isn't teaching – it's indoctrination.

We can expect to see more of this type of indoctrination if provincial curriculum guides continue to focus more on social justice than on learning a defined body of knowledge. For example, when the previous Alberta government in Canada rewrote its K–12 social studies curriculum, there was a disturbing lack of emphasis on historical facts and events. Instead, students focused on broad themes such as diversity and environmental stewardship. This ambiguity practically invites teachers to indoctrinate students.

There is a better option. In order for students to become critical thinkers, they need to master a defined body of knowledge in a variety of subject areas. It can't be assumed that students will naturally pick up the necessary knowledge while engaging in inquiry projects conducted within specific themes. For example, if students are going to grapple with major issues like climate change, they need to know a whole lot about meteorology. Much of this knowledge needs to come by direct instruction from the teacher. Otherwise it won't be learned.

All too often, critical thinking is presented as an abstract skill when it's actually highly dependent on subject-specific content knowledge. Students can't think critically about something they know nothing about.

Social justice appeals to a lot of teachers. It can be far more exciting to engage students in what seems to be an important social justice project than to painstakingly help them master basic curriculum content. However, there are no shortcuts where real learning is concerned. If students are going to become critical thinkers, they need to first learn a lot of basic facts and skills. This may not be as flashy, but it's essential to learning. Teachers must be responsible for the essentials of learning.

When this learning process is short-circuited, students are easily brainwashed. Children, particularly those in younger grades, are influenced by their teachers. If their teacher is passionate about what he learned at his latest training session, it's easy for students to simply adopt their teacher's beliefs. It may look like students are deeply engaged in the subject matter, but more often than not they're saying what they know their teachers want to hear.

Obviously, we want to develop critical thinking in schools. So, teachers need to take the time to help their students develop substantial subject-specific content knowledge. In addition, when controversial issues arise, teachers must make sure students are exposed to more than one perspective. That way, students can make up their own minds about these issues.

MORE CANADIAN HISTORY
NEEDED IN SCHOOLS

IN 2017, THE Elementary Teachers' Federation of Ontario demanded that the name of Canada's first prime minister, John A. Macdonald, be struck from all public schools in the province. More recently, Halifax's city council voted to remove the statue of Edward Cornwallis, the city's founder, that had stood downtown since 1931. Both decisions were vigorously debated at the time and public opinion remains sharply divided.

These are two separate events about two different individuals. Nevertheless, the underlying theme is the same. Both Macdonald and Cornwallis stand accused of crimes against Indigenous people. Macdonald played a role in the establishment of residential schools, while Cornwallis offered a bounty to anyone who captured or killed a Mi'kmaq person. However, they also have many defenders, since both individuals made significant contributions to their respective communities.

In order to think critically about Macdonald and Cornwallis, we need to know a lot of facts. In Macdonald's case, we need to know about the time period in which he lived, his role as prime minister, and the impact of residential schools on Indigenous people. People who know nothing about Confederation, Macdonald or residential schools are unlikely to have anything useful to contribute to this discussion.

Cornwallis was the military officer who founded Halifax in 1749. Like many other British officers of his time, Cornwallis saw nothing wrong with killing Indigenous warriors if they supported the French and appeared to be a threat to British colonists. As with Macdonald, it is necessary to know a lot about Cornwallis and the circumstances in which he lived in order to offer an informed opinion about his legacy.

There is only one place where all Canadians, regardless of where they live, have a real opportunity to acquire the historical knowledge they need to think critically about these and other issues. The vast majority of students attend school and this is where Canadian history must be taught and learned.

Unfortunately, things are not that simple. Many educators downplay the need for students to memorize specific facts, particularly since information is widely available on the internet. Instead, they want students to focus on so-called historical thinking skills through thematic study.

However, while broad-based historical themes such as change, continuity, cause, and consequence are important tools for analyzing controversial issues, they are not sufficient. Themes and overarching frameworks are useless unless they are situated within a rich knowledge base. Thus, there is still a place for teacher-led instruction and textbooks that place events in proper chronological order.

Twenty years ago, in his book *Who Killed Canadian History?* (1998), the renowned Canadian historian Jack Granatstein sounded the alarm about the lack of proper history education in schools. Granatstein argued that students were being shortchanged by social studies courses that presented a fragmented version of Canadian history. He wanted a much stronger emphasis on content knowledge that included the memorization of specific dates.

"The teaching of this content must be based on chronology, the basic tool of history ... Too much teaching in schools today takes a module of history and puts it before students to bc digested, without much awareness of how it fits within a larger context," wrote Granatstein.

Among Canada's four Western provinces, only Manitoba requires all high school students to take a Canadian history course that puts key events in a proper chronological framework. And although Saskatchewan has a mandatory Canadian studies course for Grade 12 students, it is primarily thematic in nature.

Even worse, Alberta and British Columbia do not mandate Canadian history at all. Instead, they offer social studies courses covering themes such as ideology, genocide, nationalism, and globalization. While these courses might be very interesting, they do not substitute for a rigorous and chronologically based Canadian history course.

If we want Canadians to think critically about people like Macdonald and Cornwallis, we need to ensure they know the history of their country. Critical thinking best takes place in the presence of content knowledge.

~ 3 ~

TESTS ARE GOOD FOR STUDENTS

ON JUNE 1, 1935, the UK driving test became mandatory for all drivers. From that point on, anyone who wanted to drive a car needed to pass a standardized test, which included written and in-vehicle components. With the number of drivers increasing rapidly, it didn't take long for British politicians to recognize the need to ensure that people learned how to drive safely.

No doubt the introduction of this test greatly increased the anxiety of many would-be drivers. To reassure the public, Ford Motor Company produced a promotional film, narrated by the racing driver Sir Malcolm Campbell, which explained how the driving test worked. Interestingly, Campbell begins his narration by saying, "If there is one piece of advice I would offer learners, it is: don't be nervous."

Tests have long made people nervous. Having to demonstrate your skills and knowledge in a timed test often causes anxiety. It is for this reason that many progressive educators have strongly criticized tests, particularly those that are standardized. Progressives prefer more "authentic" assessments and argue that tests provide only a limited snapshot of student achievement. This anti-testing movement has even extended to the college and university levels, where many professors shy away from high-stakes tests and exams.

However, this chapter argues that tests are not only necessary, but also good for students. The first article describes a fascinating study from Purdue University in the US, which compared students who regularly wrote tests with those who did not. Not only did the test-taking students do better, but they also retained the course material in their long-term memories. Thus, it makes sense for classroom teachers to test students on a regular basis, and not just perfunctorily a couple of times a year.

The remaining articles tackle the controversial topic of standardized testing. These tests are created by teachers and by assessment experts, written by all students at the same time, and they are externally graded. They ensure that all students are evaluated in the same way on the same curriculum. By comparing school results on these tests, education officials can identify which schools are meeting curriculum targets and which are not. As you will see in the articles, some Canadian provinces have moved toward standardized testing, while others have moved away from it. The same arguments are taking place in the US and Britain.

The articles tell the story of Prince Edward Island, a Canadian province where student achievement has risen steadily since it introduced standardized testing about 12 years ago. In contrast, in the province of Manitoba, student achievement has declined since the provincial government eliminated most standardized tests. One article praises Saskatchewan's plan to introduce standardized testing. Sadly, since that piece was published, Saskatchewan has caved in to pressure from testing opponents and backed down.

Although these cases are specific to Canada, the general principles are applicable in other countries. No doubt, readers will see that standardized testing isn't something to be feared, but rather something to be embraced. If it makes sense to require drivers to take a standardized driving test, it makes sense to expect the same of students in their academic subject areas.

PURDUE UNIVERSITY STUDY PUNCTURES THE ANTI-TESTING BUBBLE

IT IS WRONG to force students to memorize information simply because it's going to be on a test. Instead of telling students what they need to learn, teachers should encourage them to construct their own understanding of the world around them.

Anyone involved in education knows that such edu-babble statements are often heard in teacher-training institutions. Education professors continually push teachers to move away from traditional methods of instruction.

A friend of mine, who graduated several years ago with his Bachelor of Education degree, told me the main question on one of his final exams: "Explain why testing is a poor way to authentically assess student learning." The irony of testing students on their understanding of why testing is bad never seemed to sink in for that professor.

Unfortunately, this anti-testing mantra affects more than just educational theory in Canada. In the early 2000s, Manitoba eliminated most provincial standards tests, while at the school level, many administrators expected teachers to reduce their use of tests in the classroom. These administrators claimed that students benefited more from hands-on activities than from memorizing items scheduled to appear on the next test.

However, a research study published in 2011 in the journal *Science* presented a significant challenge to the reigning educational ideology. Researchers from Purdue University in the US asked 200 college students to read several paragraphs about a scientific topic, such as how the digestive system works. Students were then divided into several groups, with each group using a different study technique. The study found that students who took a test in which they wrote out the key concepts by memory significantly outperformed students who did not take a test.

A week later, the same groups of students were given a short-answer test about the material in question. Once again, the students who had studied for a test one week earlier substantially outperformed everyone else. Even the students themselves were surprised at the difference studying for a test made to their long-term retention of the subject matter. These results certainly challenge the assumption that students who study for tests simply forget the material immediately afterwards.

The lead researcher on this study, the psychology professor Jeffrey Karpicke, noted that these results confirmed the importance of actively committing concepts to memory. "But learning is fundamentally about retrieving, and our research shows that practising retrieval while you study is crucial to learning. Self-testing enriches and improves the learning process, and there needs to be more focus on using retrieval as a learning strategy," stated Karpicke.

In other words, learning, particularly in the lower grades, has more to do with acquiring knowledge than constructing knowledge. There is a core base of knowledge and skills that all students need to acquire, and schools are responsible for ensuring that this happens.

The Purdue University study lends considerable weight to the position that teachers should require their students to write tests on a regular basis. Although this does not necessitate the complete abandonment of other assessment methods, it does mean that professional development for teachers should recognize the value of traditional teaching methods.

One of the arguments commonly used against this approach is that it encourages rote learning, instead of critical thinking. The problem with this argument is that it creates a false dichotomy, since critical thinking can only take place if students possess the necessary knowledge base. For example, students who memorize their basic math facts are far better positioned to master complex mathematical concepts than those who never learn them.

In addition, if we want to help students retain the knowledge they acquire in school, it makes sense for schools to require students to write final exams in core subject areas. It is not difficult to see how the process of studying for final exams helps students to retain key concepts from their courses. None of this means that teachers should rely exclusively on making students memorize information for tests. However, we must ensure that testing remains a central component of what happens in school.

WHY NOT GAUGE PROGRESS WITH A FOLLOW-UP EXAM?

IS IT POSSIBLE to walk and chew gum at the same time? Apparently not, at least when it comes to education policy in Nova Scotia.

In the 2013–14 school year, Nova Scotia's Department of Education changed the grade levels at which standardized exams were written. The most notable change was moving math and literacy exams out of Grade 12 and into Grade 10. The provincial government defended its decision by arguing that writing the exams earlier gave schools an opportunity to correct problems identified by the assessment. That part seemed reasonable enough,

Getting reliable information about student achievement earlier in high school can help teachers to better focus their instruction. What doesn't make sense is the notion that adding standardized exams in Grade 10 necessitates their removal in Grade 12. Assessment of student learning is not a zero-sum game and there is no reason to assume that students cannot write standardized exams twice in their high school career.

It's like a car manufacturing plant adding an inspection earlier in the production process, while removing any requirement to inspect the final product. Without that check at the end, no one knows whether the car was actually built properly.

Similarly, removing Grade 12 standardized exams makes it impossible to determine whether schools have been successful in helping students to master the basics. In addition, during the transition period in Nova Scotia, no high school students wrote any standardized exams at all. Several entire grades slipped through the cracks.

Most other Canadian provinces require Grade 12 students to write standardized exams in some subjects. High-performing provinces such as Alberta and British Columbia require Grade 12 students to take standardized exams, as do Newfoundland and Labrador. Even Manitoba, the province that has systematically dismantled its standardized testing system, has chosen to keep its Grade 12 exams.

Since many high school graduates go on to post-secondary education, it is important that they are prepared for the reality that they will write many exams in college or university. Writing a provincial final exam in their last year of school is an excellent way of preparing students for what lies ahead.

The current assessment philosophy in vogue across Canada, including in Nova Scotia, is known as assessment for learning. It emphasizes the distinction between formative assessment (preliminary feedback) and summative assessment (final tests/exams). Because of this philosophy, teachers are encouraged to make assessment more about giving constructive feedback than simply measuring academic progress at the end.

When applied to standardized exams, it's not difficult to see why Nova Scotia wants students to write them at earlier grade levels, so as to better use them to inform instructional practice. What doesn't logically follow is the idea that summative assessment becomes less important. You need both formative and summative assessment. Thus, a balanced approach to the standardized exam issue would be to have students write standardized exams in grades 10 and 12.

We don't have to travel far to see how this could look. In the Chignecto-Central regional school board in Nova Scotia, students write standardized tests in Grade 10, along with the provincially mandated Grade 12 exams. Obviously, this isn't a problem, since their students have the highest academic average in the province.

The Nova Scotia government should do the right thing and reinstate the standardized exams in Grade 12. More information about student achievement is always a good thing. In this case, we can have our cake and eat it too.

SASKATCHEWAN STUDENTS CAN BENEFIT FROM MORE TESTS

SASKATCHEWAN STUDENTS SHOULD get ready to write a lot more tests. By 2016, all students in grades 4–12 will be writing yearly standardized tests in reading, writing, math, and science. This is good news for public education and, if implemented properly, should lead to improved academic achievement for Saskatchewan students.

The province currently administers some standardized tests to Saskatchewan students, but it does so only every other year. In addition, students write each test in only two or three grades. So although the current testing system provides a sample of student achievement, it is too limited in scope to have much of an impact.

A more comprehensive approach to standardized testing will benefit students in a number of ways. One is that these tests will provide the provincial government with a more accurate understanding of academic achievement throughout Saskatchewan. With this information, the province will be able to target additional support and intervention to schools with low results, and also learn from schools that get better results.

As for the concern that schools in rich neighbourhoods will automatically outperform schools in poor neighbourhoods, yearly standardized testing can do far more than simply provide raw scores. Rather, the province will be able to track improvement from year to year. So, a school in a poor neighbourhood that shows consistent achievement gains would actually be considered more successful than a school in a rich neighbourhood that remains stagnant. This type of measurement can only be done if the tests are carried out on an annual basis in all grades, as the government has proposed.

Another benefit is that standardized tests help teachers to focus their instruction on the mandated curriculum. Knowing that their students will be tested on the curriculum provides teachers with a strong incentive to cover the key concepts thoroughly. Without standardized tests in place, it is almost impossible to be sure if teachers have actually taught the complete curriculum.

Opposition to Saskatchewan's standardized testing announcement came from predictable sources. In an interview, the president of the Saskatchewan Teachers' Federation, Colin Keess, said that additional standardized tests would not help teachers to identify the strengths and weaknesses of their students. According to Keess, this was because "standardized assessments are not as useful for informing the daily practices of the teachers." This is a common sentiment among teachers' unions across Canada.

However, this objection reflects a misunderstanding of the purpose of regularly administered standardized tests. Nothing in the Saskatchewan government's announcement indicated that standardized testing was expected to take the place of the professional judgment of teachers in their classrooms. Rather, such testing helps to provide a more complete picture of student achievement across the province.

In fact, both teacher-created assessment and standardized testing are essential for a balanced approach to student assessment. Teacher-created assessment ensures teachers can take individual student needs into account when designing and evaluating assignments and tests. Standardized testing introduces systematic balance with an objective measurement tool that makes it possible to determine whether provincial curriculum standards have been met.

Another objection was raised by Patrick Lewis, a professor in the University of Regina's education faculty. According to the *Regina Leader-Post*, Lewis argued that standardized testing provides only a snapshot of student performance and not a complete picture of overall achievement. He also expressed concern that teachers would simply teach to the test.

However, this concern can be addressed by making sure such tests are properly correlated with the provincial curriculum. It makes sense to ensure that the tests are broad in scope and go beyond an assessment of basic skills. One way to do this is for the tests to also measure content knowledge in the various subject areas. This should reduce the temptation for schools to sacrifice important subjects such as science and social studies when preparing for these tests.

As part of the announcement, Saskatchewan's education minister, Russ Marchuk, explained that 13 teachers from across the province would be responsible for designing the tests. While it makes sense to give local teachers significant input into the design of these tests, it is also important to include measurement experts in the design process. For example, Alberta has the most advanced standardized testing system in Canada and officials in its education department could give valuable input about the proper design of these tests.

If designed and implemented properly, standardized testing can result in a better education for the students of Saskatchewan.

This article was originally published in 2013. Saskatchewan has since dropped plans to introduce standardized testing

STANDARDIZED TESTING IS NEEDED NOW

WHEN THE RESULTS of the 2012 Programme for International Student Assessment (PISA) were published, things didn't look good for Manitoba.

Every three years, PISA tests more than 500,000 15-year-old students from approximately 65 countries in the core competency areas of math, reading, and science. Students from all Canadian provinces participate in the tests. Compared with other provinces, Manitoba's students ranked near the bottom in 2012. To make matters worse, the decline continued a trend that had begun more than a decade earlier.

In what looked like an obvious attempt at deflection, the province's Department of Education sent out a flurry of press releases trumpeting some of its education initiatives, on the same day that the PISA results were released. Smaller class sizes, back-to-basics math instruction, and new report cards all featured prominently. Clearly, the Manitoba government wanted parents and taxpayers to believe that everything was under control in its public schools: don't worry about the declining performance of our students, look at all the good things that are happening!

Some of the initiatives did have promise. Most notably, changes to the K–8 math curriculum – requiring students to memorize math facts and use the standard algorithms for addition, subtraction, multiplication, and division – would, no doubt, improve the math skills of students. The research literature, however, is inconclusive on whether class-size caps and new report cards make much difference to student academic achievement. Instead of engaging in a snow job, the Department of Education should have answered one fundamental question: how would it evaluate the effectiveness of these and other education initiatives?

Commonly used criteria such as high school graduation rates, attendance rates, and student attitude surveys don't really tell parents and taxpayers much about academic achievement. But there is a better option. Manitoba could have followed the lead of every other Canadian province and brought back standardized testing. Before 1999, Manitoba students wrote standardized tests in grades 3, 6, 9, and 12. With the exception of the Grade 12 tests, these tests have been systematically eliminated. And, interestingly, the elimination of standardized testing closely coincided with the steady decline in Manitoba students' achievement in the PISA tests.

Annual standardized tests at a few grade levels would make it possible to measure the effectiveness of new education initiatives. Instead of waiting three years until the next PISA test, Manitoba should have created its own tests based on the provincial curriculum.

With information obtained from properly designed standardized tests, the government could have reacted more quickly when problems were identified. Provincial tests can also identify areas of excellence.

One of the most common arguments against standardized tests is that those countries that have them, such as the US, have worse PISA results. There are two major problems with this argument. First, the standardized tests used in Canadian provinces bear almost no resemblance to the US tests. The narrowly defined, high-stakes exams used in many US states are much different than the balanced, curriculum-based tests used in higher-performing provinces. Second, most of the top-performing countries in PISA (such as Singapore, Japan, and South Korea) have standardized testing in place. Overall, the results show that well-designed standardized tests can benefit student academic performance.

Without standardized tests to keep them focused on the fundamentals, schools often drift away from an academic focus. From school division amalgamations to extra physical education credits and social justice initiatives, Manitoba's Department of Education has focused on everything except improving the academic achievement of its students. Receiving a wake-up call every three years from the PISA results isn't enough to make the department change course.

In order to move up from the bottom of the pack, Manitoba's schools need a sharper focus on the academic basics. This will only happen if parents and taxpayers force the department to measure academic results with standardized tests. Without this accountability, the province will continue to drift aimlessly.

CHALLENGING THE ARGUMENTS AGAINST STANDARDIZED TESTS

ALFIE KOHN, A hard-core progressive, is one of the most controversial education writers in North America today. It isn't hard to see why. Kohn opposes not only standardized tests, but also teacher-created tests and even assignments. He doesn't think students should receive grades and he supports no-fail policies, believes teachers should not try to control their students, and criticizes any form of direct instruction.

Hopefully, some teachers can see through Kohn's rhetoric and examine the evidence themselves. In fact, there are many reasons why teachers should support, rather than oppose, standardized testing.

Perhaps the most important reason is that standardized tests make it possible to measure academic achievement. Because all students write the same test on the same day, the results are more reliable than the results of teacher-created tests, which vary widely depending on each teacher. This does not mean that teacher-created tests are unimportant. Rather, they simply need to be balanced with standardized tests in order to get a true picture of student academic achievement.

Another benefit of standardized testing is that it helps teachers to focus their instruction on the mandated curriculum. Knowing that their students will be tested on the curriculum provides teachers with a strong incentive to cover the material thoroughly.

For provincial governments to set meaningful targets for academic skills such as reading, writing, and math, some form of standardized testing is essential. Otherwise, there is no way of knowing whether students have learned the curriculum. Parents send their children to school with the expectation that they will learn specific knowledge and skills. Standardized testing holds teachers and principals accountable for meeting these expectations.

One of the arguments commonly made by opponents of standardized tests is that they are biased against students from minority groups and from disadvantaged backgrounds. There are two main problems with this argument. First, if it is possible to identify examples of bias on standardized tests, it is also possible to correct these biases. Rather than simply throwing out the entire test because of a few examples of bias, why not make the necessary adjustments to ensure that the tests are fair?

The second major problem with this argument is that it seems to question the ability of teachers to help all students learn the curriculum. Teachers regularly provide special assistance to students who are disadvantaged because of their linguistic or cultural experiences, and it is reasonable to think that this assistance will be provided when disadvantaged students are preparing to write standardized tests.

Another common argument against standardized testing is that it is too costly and the money could be better spent elsewhere. However, this argument also fails to withstand scrutiny. In Nova Scotia, for example, the evaluation services division of the Department of

Education is responsible for standardized testing. It has a total annual budget of approximately CA$2.7 million. To put this amount into perspective, the entire Department of Education has a total annual budget of just over CA$1.2 billion.

In other words, standardized testing would make up only 0.2% of total education spending in Nova Scotia. It seems reasonable to spend 0.2% of the education budget on a reliable evaluation of academic achievement. Eliminating standardized testing in the name of reducing costs makes about as much sense as removing diagnostic equipment from hospitals in order to save money.

PROVINCIAL ACHIEVEMENT TESTS ARE STILL IMPORTANT

EVERY YEAR, THOUSANDS of students in Alberta take driver education classes in hopes of passing the all-important written and practical driving test. These classes are taught through a traditional, teacher-centred approach, in which driving instructors teach students the rules of the road and show them how to drive on provincial roadways. It's old-fashioned, but it works.

Suppose the people in charge decided to radically overhaul driver education. After all, students couldn't possibly learn how to drive 21st-century cars using 20th-century driver education strategies. So, government officials change all driver education programs to a "discovery" approach, where instructors no longer teach but allow students to learn how to drive on their own.

Now imagine that after several years of "discovery driver education," the percentage of students passing the driving test declines precipitously. Instead of admitting that their discovery approach was wrong, driver education administrators blame the test by claiming it is faulty. After all, the test is stressful to students, provides only a snapshot of their performance and is a poor assessment of their actual driving ability. In response to pressure, the government gradually phases out the unfair test and a golden age of driving dawns in Alberta.

Of course, everyone should realize that this scenario is patently ridiculous. It would be the height of foolishness to radically overhaul driver education for the sake of an instructional theory and then, when the test proves the theory doesn't work, blame the test rather than the theory. But that is exactly what is happening in Alberta education.

Alberta's curriculum guides have recently undergone their biggest overhaul in decades. As part of its commitment to so-called 21st-century learning, the provincial government has reduced academic content and placed more emphasis on the process of learning, even though considerable research shows that generic learning skills, such as critical thinking, cannot be mastered without substantial content knowledge.

Discovery math is a case in point. Despite grandiose promises made by discovery math advocates, student results on provincial achievement tests (PATs) have steadily declined over the past few years. Results have revealed that more than a quarter of Grade 6 students and nearly a third of Grade 9 students failed to meet the provincial standard of proficiency.

However, organizations favouring discovery learning blame PATs, rather than the faulty approach to math education. For example, the Alberta Teachers' Association wants PATs phased out entirely because it believes the tests are too stressful for students, do not measure what is really important, and cost too much money to administer.

Too bad those arguments are specious. Although students may experience some stress before writing a test, this is a normal part of the educational experience, and a normal part of life. In addition, while PATs are not perfect, they are closely correlated to the curriculum and are considered by expert psychometricians to be reliable and valid. As for the cost, PATs make up a tiny fraction of the provincial education budget. Eliminating them would not free up much money for other things.

The key value of PATs is in measuring student achievement across the province. Without PATs, Alberta would have no way of tracking trends in student achievement or identifying schools that need additional support. The goal of PATs is not to evaluate teacher performance, but rather to determine whether students are adequately mastering the foundational knowledge and skills. When problems are accurately diagnosed, they can be addressed and corrected.

For example, the provincial government recently made some positive revisions to the math curriculum by requiring students to memorize the multiplication tables and solve simple math problems without using calculators. Although these changes did not go nearly far enough, they likely would not have happened at all had the PATs not shown the clear failure of the discovery method.

Unfortunately, previous governments in Alberta have systematically undermined the PATs with the end goal of removing them altogether. From lowering the value of Grade 12 diploma exams, to eliminating Grade 3 PATs, to doubling the length of time students can take to write each exam, successive governments have sent a message that PATs are a low priority at best and harmful at worst. This is unfortunate.

Just as the driving test remains an important way of evaluating prospective drivers, PATs are an essential component of student assessment. The Alberta government should strengthen rather than undermine them.

This article was originally published in 2017. In the spring of 2019,
a new provincial government was elected in Alberta

IMPROVING STUDENT ACHIEVEMENT IN PRINCE EDWARD ISLAND

THE RESULTS FROM the 2016 Pan-Canadian Assessment Program (PCAP) reveal that students in Prince Edward Island (PEI) scored among the highest in the country. This is impressive, but it seems even more so when we remember that a decade ago PEI ranked at the bottom of Canadian provinces.

One should not read too much into the results of one assessment, particularly since the PCAP measures only a sample of Grade 8 students. However, PEI has made similar gains in the Programme for International Student Assessment (PISA), which also takes place every three years. When two separate standardized assessment instruments show similar results, there is good reason to take the information seriously.

PEI's gains on the PISA and PCAP assessments coincide almost precisely with the introduction of provincial standardized testing. Before 2007, PEI students wrote no standardized exams and ranked near the bottom in student achievement in Canada. Since the province introduced standardized testing in several grade levels, student achievement has substantially improved.

It isn't hard to see why standardized testing makes a difference. Simply put, it ensures that curriculum outcomes are taught. It is too easy for school administrators to introduce numerous initiatives that teachers know burn their time to cover the entire curriculum. Standardized testing gives teachers the incentive to push back on fads, and to point out that students need to prepare for provincial standardized tests.

Unfortunately, the PEI Teachers' Federation continues to oppose standardized testing. In particular, the federation thinks the provincial government should scrap these tests and use the money to improve classroom conditions. The problem with this proposal is that the PEI government spends only CA$1.2 million on assessment each year. With a total annual budget of about CA$274 million, standardized testing makes up less than 0.5% of the education budget. While standardized testing appears to have a big impact on student achievement, its impact on the budget is tiny. Clearly, the provincial government should continue with the standardized testing program.

However, the PEI government needs to do more. In order to make further improvements in student achievement, the government needs to revise the curriculum and place greater emphasis on subject-specific content knowledge. Like other provinces, PEI is heavily influenced by the 21st-century skills movement.

This movement, represented in Canada by the organization C21 Canada, believes it is more important to teach students so-called transferable skills than to help them acquire content knowledge. Because the world is changing so quickly, C21 advocates claim there is no point in students memorizing facts that will soon be outdated. Rather, students should learn what the Ontario education guru Michael Fullan calls the six Cs: character, citizenship, collaboration, critical thinking, communication, and creativity.

However, the six Cs omit the most important C of all – content. Every subject has specific knowledge that students need to master, and without that content, students cannot think critically about a subject, communicate effectively about it, or collaborate meaningfully with others. Unless students have content knowledge, the six Cs are useless.

Math is one of the subjects hit hardest by this approach. In 2015, the Toronto-based C. D. Howe Institute published a report authored by the math professor Anna Stokke, which pointed out that math curricula across Canada placed too little emphasis on direct learning strategies such as memorizing multiplication tables and practicing long division. PEI education officials cannot afford to be complacent. In the latest PCAP results, math was the one subject where PEI students scored below the national average.

Another reason to increase content knowledge in the curriculum is that it directly influences reading comprehension. Many research studies confirm that students with prior background knowledge of the topic of an article or book are most likely to be able to understand what they read. This means that students need to learn as much as possible in as many subjects as they can. Instead of reducing content in the curriculum, education officials need to increase it.

Thus, PEI needs to do two things in order to further improve student achievement: keep standardized tests in place, even though the Teachers' Federation is against them, and revise all the provincial curriculum guides to reflect a knowledge-rich emphasis. PEI students deserve nothing less.

~4~

CONTENT KNOWLEDGE IS IMPORTANT

J.R.R. TOLKIEN IS mainly remembered today as the author of the magnificent *The Lord of the Rings* trilogy. Anyone who reads *The Lord of the Rings* cannot help but be impressed by the depth of the narrative and the incredible history of Middle-earth, the fictional continent where events unfold. What starts as a relatively simple account of how a young hobbit acquires a magic ring quickly transforms into an epic battle of good versus evil.

What sets Tolkien apart from other fantasy writers is not just his style, but also the breadth of his creation. He doesn't just write a story, he imagines a whole new world complete with its own unique history. In this fantasy world, one finds new creatures, new languages, and new kingdoms. Tolkien spent years mapping out the history of Middle-earth and took pride in what he had created.

Tolkien showed a tremendous amount of creativity in his writings. However, he had something else that was even more important – content knowledge. He had a solid university education in philology (the study of languages) and developed an impressive expertise in Old English literature. Anyone familiar with Norse mythologies can see the significant impact they had on Tolkien's writing. Without this extensive content knowledge, he could never have created Middle-earth, no matter how creative he might have been.

In today's schools, we hear a lot about the importance of critical thinking and creativity, but far less about the significance of content knowledge. This is deeply unfortunate, since content knowledge makes critical thinking and creativity possible. The first article in this chapter tells the story of my encounter with an education professor in Atlantic Canada who genuinely believes there is no single piece of information that all students should know. Sadly, this dismissive approach to content knowledge is more common in education circles than most people realize.

The remaining articles make the case for the importance of content knowledge in all subject areas. My key arguments are that content knowledge is necessary for reading comprehension, it makes critical thinking possible, and it narrows the gap between rich and poor students. Contrary to what progressive educators claim, students cannot simply rely on Google to provide them with the information or knowledge they need. Content knowledge needs to be directly taught – and it needs to be taught by teachers.

While most students probably won't become writers like J.R.R. Tolkien, all of them can benefit from a stronger focus on content knowledge in schools.

EDU-BABBLE ON THE EAST COAST

DURING SPRING BREAK in 2012, I had the opportunity to travel to the east coast of Canada for a speaking tour. As part of its AIMS on Campus initiative, the Atlantic Institute for Market Studies had arranged for me to speak to education students and professors at several universities.

The most memorable encounter took place at Acadia University in Wolfville, Nova Scotia. Interestingly, the faculty of education had arranged for two members of their department to deliver a formal rebuttal immediately after my presentation. Since I welcome debate, this condition was not a problem, although it made me wonder whether they follow this procedure for all their guest speakers.

During my 30-minute presentation, I made my usual case for a more traditional approach to education. I emphasized the importance of content in the curriculum, argued for a sharper focus on basic skills, and defended standardized testing as a useful measurement tool.

Immediately after my presentation, Dr. Michael Corbett, a professor of education at Acadia, delivered his response. He started out by identifying himself as a romantic progressive and said he disagreed with almost everything I said. He then talked about his upbringing in rural Nova Scotia and said he came from a low-income family. Most of his siblings did not finish school and Corbett laid the blame directly at the feet of a system that was, in his view, too academically focused. "Standardized testing ruined my family," he complained.

His comments went downhill from there. He stated that I should not have referred to the Canadian education system, since there actually is no such thing. However, when he later talked about international assessments that make our country look good, he referred multiple times to the "Canadian education system" and downplayed the many significant differences between the provinces. It struck me as a rather obvious inconsistency on his part.

Corbett also claimed it was impossible to identify any specific knowledge that every student should know. In his view, all knowledge is subjective and prescribing specific content in the curriculum is problematic.

The second rebuttal was delivered by a doctoral education student who made many of the same arguments as Corbett. She zeroed in on the issue of core knowledge and said we need not worry about content in the curriculum. Apparently, teachers should let students decide for themselves what knowledge is of most worth.

Frankly, I found it incredible that education "experts" could deny something as simple as the premise that there are some facts all students should learn. When I asked them if it would be OK for students to learn nothing about Canadian Confederation throughout their time in school, they actually had to sit and think for a while because they weren't sure how to respond. Fortunately, the dean said she agreed with me that everyone should learn about Confederation.

Then one of the undergraduate education students spoke up and categorically stated that all of his education courses were a complete waste of time. He said education professors presented only one side of the issue during discussions, didn't challenge students academically, and often assigned meaningless reflection papers. Needless to say, the education professors didn't seem pleased with his comments.

Interestingly, he was not the only education student to express this view. Another student spoke up during the discussion and backed up the first student's comments. When I talked privately with them afterwards, other students added that their education courses were completely useless.

AIMS is providing a much-needed service to university students. Edu-babble is deeply entrenched in education faculties and the AIMS on Campus program makes it possible for education students to hear an alternative perspective.

CANADIAN HISTORY MUST BE TAUGHT IN SCHOOLS

THE FORMER CANADIAN prime minister William Lyon Mackenzie King once said, "If some countries have too much history, we have too much geography." He implied that because of the relatively young age of our country, Canada has less history than most other countries.

However, having a shorter history is no guarantee that our citizens are more likely to know it well.

In a 2009 survey commissioned by the Dominion Institute, less than half of Canadians aged 18–35 could identify John A. Macdonald, Canada's first prime minister, from his portrait. Fewer than one in ten could identify Tommy Douglas, the first leader of the New Democratic Party, and barely one in five recognized the Métis leader Louis Riel. Even the former prime minister Pierre Trudeau was unknown by almost half of Canadians in the same cohort.

In 2011, the federal minister of citizenship and immigration introduced a new citizenship guide. In order to be granted citizenship, applicants must now demonstrate sufficient knowledge of essential Canadian history. The 64-page study guide, *Discover Canada*, devotes ten pages to a chronological overview of key events in our history. Any applicant who does not master these facts cannot pass the citizenship test.

Since we expect new citizens to be familiar with Canadian history, it makes sense to apply the same standard to those who grow up in this country. This is why most people expect schools to ensure that students learn the key events in Canadian history.

While there will always be debate around which historical events are most important, it's not difficult to identify some fundamental things that everyone should know. For example, few would dispute that all Canadians should be familiar with our Confederation of 1867, Samuel de Champlain's founding of Quebec City in 1608, Canada's contribution during the two world wars, and the patriation of the Constitution in 1982. Dark chapters of our history – such as Indigenous residential schools, the Chinese head tax, and the forced relocation of Japanese Canadians during World War II – should also be studied.

Understanding our past, warts and all, makes us better able to grapple with the issues confronting our country today. A well-educated and broadly informed general public is the best protection against misguided government policies. Knowing our past makes it easier for us to build on our successes and avoid repeating our failures.

Because education is a provincial responsibility, there are no national history standards. Unfortunately, most provinces fail to provide an adequate history curriculum to public school students – a fact well-documented by the renowned historian Jack Granatstein in his book *Who Killed Canadian History?* (1998).

Although every province includes some Canadian history in the elementary grades, most do not require high school students to take a full course on the subject, instead prescribing nebulous social studies courses. For example, Alberta students take courses in globalization, nationalism, and ideology, while British Columbia students take a Grade 12 history course in which they look at major world events of the 20th century. Neither province mandates a high school course in Canadian history.

Saskatchewan does require Grade 12 students to take a history course called Canadian studies. Unfortunately, the course is arranged thematically rather than chronologically. Instead of starting at a chosen point and showing how one historical event builds on another, students jump from topics such as "External forces and domestic realities" to "The forces of nationalism."

Interestingly, Manitoba stands out as a bright light among the provinces. Not only are all Manitoba's Grade 11 students required to take Canadian history, but the course content is arranged chronologically. Furthermore, the new textbook that goes with the curriculum provides a useful and easy-to-read overview of key events in Canadian history. Other provinces would do well to follow Manitoba's example.

Much of the inadequate teaching of history in our schools stems from a faulty educational philosophy. Prospective teachers are told by their education professors not to focus on making sure students learn a core knowledge base, but rather to emphasize the so-called process of learning. As a result, schools focus on abstract concepts such as globalization, nationalism, and social justice at the expense of specific knowledge and skills.

Canadian history is too important a subject for us to allow it to fall out of use. No student should graduate from high school without a solid understanding of the events that have shaped our great country.

IN EDUCATION, CONTENT SHOULD BE KING

SUPPOSE YOU JOIN a discussion about something you know nothing about. How much weight will your opinion receive? Probably not much. Even if you follow proper conversation strategies such as remaining on topic and keeping your comments respectful, your input will not be valued when you are completely ignorant about the subject at hand. Most people recognize that content knowledge is essential in most discussions.

Knowledge is also important in areas such as reading. If you read a newspaper or magazine article about hockey, you are likely to understand it if you are familiar with the rules of hockey. In contrast, someone who knows nothing about hockey will probably not benefit much from reading about last night's game. If you need to Google basic hockey terms such as offside, icing, or penalty box, your background knowledge of hockey is likely insufficient to understand the article properly.

The importance of content is strongly supported by experts such as the cognitive psychologist Daniel Willingham. He regularly conducts research on the role of consciousness in learning and has found that background knowledge makes it easier for us to learn, as it frees up space in our working memory for tackling new concepts.

Given the importance of broad-based factual knowledge, it is imperative that schools ensure students become knowledgeable citizens. However, this is unlikely to happen when some of the best-known thinkers in education regularly downplay the importance of knowledge and focus instead on the so-called process of learning.

Alfie Kohn, for example, is a well-known author and speaker who opposes any attempt to make content the focus of the curriculum, which he derides as the "bunch o' facts" approach to education. His books are widely influential among teachers and he is regularly invited to speak at teacher professional development sessions.

The romantic progressive ideology promoted by Kohn is widely taught in the education faculties that train teachers. It should come as little surprise that this idcology influences the standards contained in provincial curriculum guides. As a case in point, English language arts (ELA) curriculum guides contain lots of edu-babble but not much content.

Their extensive length and verbosity notwithstanding, most ELA curriculum guides are little more than empty shells. While these guides encourage students to "enhance the clarity and artistry of communication" and "celebrate and build community," most do not prescribe any specific books or authors for all students to read. As a result, schools miss out on the opportunity to ensure that all students share some common background knowledge.

Fortunately, some educators are pushing back against this worrisome trend. In his book *Focus: Elevating the Essentials to Radically Improve Student Learning* (2011), former school administrator Mike Schmoker skewers ELA curriculum guides for their "bloated, confusing, [and] poorly written" standards. He concludes that "language arts, more than any other discipline, has lost its way," and proposes the removal of meaningless verbiage from ELA curriculum guides. Schmoker says curriculum guides should list the titles of books and articles each student must read, specify the number and length of papers required, and identify the evaluation criteria for student work.

This does not mean teachers should lose all teaching discretion. In fact, Schmoker and other advocates of core knowledge, such as E. D. Hirsch, Jr., suggest that only about half of the reading materials and assignments need to be prescribed by the curriculum. Teachers should select the other half. This approach appropriately balances teacher professional autonomy with the need to uphold a consistent standard for all students.

Schmoker offers a similar critique of curriculum guides in science and social studies. He notes that the excessive use of hands-on experiments in science means students spend too little time reading and thinking about important scientific concepts. As for social studies, Schmoker contends that curriculum guides in that subject are often filled with meaningless verbiage that obscures important historical content. This is unacceptable.

The best way to prepare students for the 21st century is to make sure they are immersed in a content-rich curriculum that provides them with the background knowledge they need. This will only happen if we move away from the failed romantic progressive ideology and adopt an approach that restores content to its rightful place. When it comes to 21st-century education, content should be king.

EDUCATORS HAVE IT BACKWARDS ON FACTUAL LEARNING

IMAGINE YOU ARE a fly on the wall in a faculty of education classroom or a teacher professional development session. What would you hear? Chances are that you would hear about the need for teachers to establish a student-centred classroom environment in which a hands-on discovery approach prevails. Teachers are regularly told to focus more on the so-called process of learning than on specific academic content.

The degree to which factual knowledge is de-emphasized and even disparaged in education circles usually comes as a surprise to most parents and taxpayers. After all, school is generally assumed to be a place where students learn specific knowledge and skills so they eventually become productive citizens.

Instead, teachers are told in faculties of education and professional development sessions that they are simply "guides on the side" who facilitate the creation of new knowledge by students. This is where failed innovations such as fuzzy math, whole language, and open-area classrooms find their root. At their heart is a bizarre notion that there is little need to impart specific factual knowledge to students.

However, despite the widespread acceptance of this ideology by education professors and education department officials, there is remarkably little evidence supporting it. In fact, the weight of the research evidence comes down squarely on the side of those who advocate for the direct instruction of specific factual knowledge.

In their book *Visible Learning and the Science of How We Learn* (2014), the educational researcher John Hattie and the cognitive psychologist Gregory Yates do not mince words when they say, "There is little basis to suggest that personal discovery within itself assists a person to actually learn … The discovery learning process demands a high level of non-productive mental effort, which could be more profitably directed to genuine knowledge building."

Far from being irrelevant pieces of trivia, factual knowledge provides students with the essential building blocks that make higher-level learning possible. It is not hard to see why this is so. Take two students, one who knows many facts about the Métis leader Louis Riel and another who has never heard anything about him. It shouldn't take too long to figure out which student is more likely to develop a deep understanding of the historical grievances of the Métis people.

The same principle holds true in other subject areas. Mathematics is an obvious case in point. A student who knows his multiplication tables by memory is far more likely to succeed at solving algebraic equations than a student who needs a calculator to answer basic questions such as 5 x 6. This is because the student who does not know the multiplication tables is more likely to become bogged down and confused by sequential, multi-step problems.

Cognitive psychologists have developed a term for this important concept: cognitive load, which means there is a limit to the amount of information that can be easily stored in our working memory. This is why, for example, we usually struggle to remember a newly introduced seven-digit phone number. However, once a phone number has been committed to long-term memory through frequent repetition, we no longer have difficulty remembering it. Because the phone number is now recalled automatically, it produces a very low cognitive load. The same holds true with the subject knowledge taught in school. Students who know their basic math facts experience less cognitive load when solving advanced math problems than students who do not.

In his book *Why Don't Students Like School?* (2009), the cognitive psychologist Daniel Willingham summarizes the importance of factual knowledge: "The very processes that teachers care about most – critical thinking processes such as reasoning and problem solving – are intimately intertwined with factual knowledge that is stored in long-term memory (not just found in the environment)."

In other words, students cannot think critically about a major historical event if they know nothing about the event in question. Nor can they solve multi-step algebraic equations without knowing the correct order of operations. A broad knowledge base is absolutely essential to the development of critical thinking skills.

Thus, despite what prospective teachers may hear from their education professors, students benefit greatly when their teachers directly impart knowledge to them. In order for students to think critically, they must become knowledgeable first.

KNOWLEDGE LEADS TO
THE PROMISED LAND

EVER TRY TO argue with someone who is totally ignorant about a topic but still convinced he is right? I have. Believe me when I say it is a frustrating experience. There is only so much you can say to someone who rejects your position as "stupid" despite knowing nothing about it. Ignorance is not a good thing.

In a 2015 online post, the Humanists, Atheists, and Agnostics of Manitoba (HAAM) made the rather serious allegation that some Manitoba schools were producing ignorant graduates. Much of HAAM's concern stemmed from the fact that some private religious schools were allegedly teaching their students about creationism and that a significant number of Manitoba university students did not believe in the theory of evolution. HAAM said it was unfortunate that "a student could go all the way through school and never be taught Darwinian evolution."

On this issue HAAM are partly right and partly wrong. They are right that all high school graduates should have an accurate understanding of the theory of evolution. However, they are wrong when they assume that anyone who disagrees with this theory is scientifically illiterate. In other words, it is entirely possible for someone who is familiar with all of the evidence to still reject the prevailing scientific consensus on this or any other issue.

To illustrate, let's consider four hypothetical students. Student A accepts evolution, but cannot provide any supporting arguments or even explain what it is. Student B accepts evolution and can accurately explain the theory and respond to counterarguments. Student C rejects evolution because he thinks it is stupid, but cannot give any other reason. Student D rejects evolution, but holds an accurate understanding of the theory and can give clear reasons for his position. Which of the above students are ignorant?

In my view, the answer is obvious. Students A and C are ignorant because they cannot give any intelligent reasons for their position. In contrast, students B and D are well-informed because they are able to support their beliefs with coherent arguments. There wouldn't be much point in students A and C having a discussion about evolution, since neither would have anything useful to contribute. On the other hand, students B and D could probably learn from each other, since they both know a lot about the topic at hand.

In one of their official position statements, HAAM say it is important to improve the quality of public education by "encouraging the development of critical thinking skills." I agree with this statement. However, this is only one half of the picture. Critical thinking skills cannot be taught in isolation, but must be developed in the context of accurate and extensive information. Without knowledge, it is impossible to think critically.

Not only does ignorance make it hard to have an intelligent conversation, but it can also prevent someone from acquiring the information they need to become better informed. That's because there is a strong correlation between reading comprehension and background knowledge. Students who know something about the topic of an article or book are more likely to comprehend the text than those who know nothing about it. Thus, when education professors downplay the importance of academic content, they are sowing the seeds of ignorance.

THERE'S NO CRITICAL THINKING WITHOUT KNOWLEDGE

THE 2016 PRESIDENTIAL election campaign was one of the worst in US history. As the two candidates slugged it out, neither showed much interest in intelligent engagement. In many ways, it was a campaign of ignorance. Fortunately, there is a remedy for ignorance – the promotion of knowledge.

Knowledge is powerful because it combats ignorance. It is a lot harder to hold on to misguided beliefs or inaccurate stereotypes when presented with cold, hard facts. Election campaigns based on ignorance are likely to become the norm, because public schools in the US are more interested in trendy fads than in the knowledge that students desperately need.

However, Canadians cannot be complacent. While our situation is better, surveys commissioned by Historica Canada reveal significant gaps in young people's knowledge about history. As a case in point, in 2015 more than one in four Canadians could not identify the name of our first prime minister and a similar number did not know that Confederation took place in 1867. This is unacceptable.

All Canadian high school graduates should have a clear understanding of the key events, dates, and people in Canadian history. For example, everyone should know about the treaties made between the First Nations and the Crown, the circumstances that led to Confederation in 1867, and Canada's involvement in the two world wars. We must identify the core knowledge that all students need to possess when they graduate and then structure the curriculum around this knowledge.

Core knowledge also includes specific scientific facts and theories that all students must know. It is unconscionable that anyone would graduate from high school without at least a basic understanding of meteorology, plate tectonics, and astronomy. Similarly, students must learn how to do basic math and be able to use these skills to solve everyday problems. As for social studies, students should at least understand what parliamentary democracy is and how it works in Canada.

Unfortunately, the 21st-century learning fad has reduced emphasis on knowledge. Trite phrases such as "the world is changing faster than ever before" and "we need to prepare students for jobs that don't yet exist" are used to defend an educational philosophy that de-emphasizes factual content and replaces it with a nebulous process of learning. While the advocates of 21st-century learning claim to value critical thinking, they fail to recognize that critical thinking can only take place when you know something about a subject. This is why core knowledge is important.

Knowledge is also the key to reading comprehension. All too often, educators think of reading as a transferable skill that can be taught in isolation from specific content. However, research shows that reading comprehension soars when students have background knowledge of the topic. If someone needs to look up the meaning of every other word in an article, that person will probably not even try reading it.

The education author E. D. Hirsch, Jr., makes this point abundantly clear in his book *Why Knowledge*

Matters: Rescuing Our Children from Failed Educational Theories (2016). Hirsch presents considerable research evidence showing that reading comprehension is closely linked to background knowledge. For many students, particularly those living in poverty, school is the only place where they can get this required knowledge. It is the only path to success for poor children.

So-called critical thinking skills do not exist in a vacuum. In far too many cases, schools attempt to get around the need for knowledge by teaching students generic comprehension strategies, such as "finding the main idea," "drawing logical inferences," and "close reading." Hirsch shows that these strategies are not a substitute for background knowledge.

Facts and knowledge are not obsolete in the 21st century – they are more important than ever. The best way to help students become critical thinkers is to make sure they acquire as much knowledge about as many subjects as possible. This will only happen when schools put knowledge at the forefront. If we want students to become productive, mature citizens, then we need to help them become knowledgeable. That is the cure for ignorance.

WHAT IS THE FOUNDATION OF QUALITY EDUCATION?

CONTENT-RICH INSTRUCTION MAY not be as flashy as some of the educational alternatives, but it's a whole lot more effective.

Educators have long debated the importance of specific content knowledge in the curriculum. Progressive educators generally favour a non-content-specific learning process. Traditional educators say all students should master a defined body of knowledge.

With its emphasis on non-content-specific skills such as critical thinking and creativity, 21st-century learning is the latest manifestation of the progressive approach. A number of Canadian provinces – notably Alberta, British Columbia and Ontario – are making substantial curriculum changes to reflect the priorities of the 21st-century learning movement. If this trend continues, content knowledge will receive less emphasis in schools.

This shift away from content knowledge should give all Canadians cause for concern, because such knowledge is essential in all subject areas and at all grade levels. There are several reasons why.

First, content knowledge is needed for reading comprehension. Give students an article to read on a topic they know nothing about and they will struggle to understand it. But they will have little difficulty reading an article or book when they possess background knowledge about the topic. The more they already know, the more effectively they can read and understand. Reading comprehension depends on background knowledge.

Second, content knowledge makes critical thinking possible. In many schools, the development of critical thinking skills is considered more important than the acquisition of specific content knowledge. However, this overlooks the fact that critical thinking can't take place in the absence of specific content knowledge.

As a case in point, consider the recent proposal by the Elementary Teachers' Federation of Ontario to remove John A. Macdonald's name from public schools. Is this a good idea or not?

In order to think critically about this question, you need to know a lot of things about Macdonald and the cultural context he lived in. Macdonald is considered a father of Confederation because of the very important role he played in bridging the divide between anglophones and francophones in mid-19th-century Canada. He also spearheaded the construction of the CPR railroad, which brought additional provinces into Confederation, and fiercely protected our country from American military aggression. These are significant accomplishments.

At the same time, Macdonald was a deeply flawed man. He drank too much, took bribes from railroad companies, brazenly handed out plum patronage jobs to his political cronies, and created a residential school system that harmed many Indigenous people. These flaws cannot be ignored. Rather, they must be weighed against his accomplishments.

People can't think critically about something they know nothing about. Although subject-specific content knowledge doesn't guarantee critical thinking, it's a prerequisite for critical thinking to take place.

Finally, content knowledge empowers students from disadvantaged backgrounds. Far too many students come to school from homes where they haven't received the same learning opportunities as their more affluent classmates. They enter school at a significant disadvantage. However, schools can largely compensate for this gap by ensuring that all students receive content-rich instruction from an early age. Content-rich instruction is key to empowering students from disadvantaged backgrounds.

Protecting content knowledge in Canadian schools begins with provincial education departments. Instead of reducing or downplaying the subject content, those who write curriculum guides must ensure that content at all grade levels is substantial and logically sequential. Whether the subject is math, science, English language arts or social studies, there's no excuse for providing teachers with nearly content-free curriculum guides. And at the local level, superintendents and principals should set a tone of support for content-rich instruction.

Students deserve the best education teachers can provide. Knowledge is powerful and good teachers know how to make their subjects come alive. By restoring knowledge to its rightful place, we can help to ensure that all students receive a top-quality education.

READING COMPREHENSION DEPENDS ON CONTENT KNOWLEDGE

WALK INTO AN elementary-school classroom and you'll probably see a lot of books on the shelf. Take a closer look and you'll often find a coloured dot, a number, or a letter on each book's spine. Those dots, numbers, and letters show the reading level of each book.

Books are assigned levels so students can choose the ones that will challenge them without being too difficult. Instead of having the entire class read the same book, students pick books from their designated reading levels. Levelled libraries make it possible for students to find the best books to read. At least, that's the theory. The reality may be somewhat different.

In order for students to read a text effectively, they must be able to do two things: decode the individual words, and comprehend the sentences and paragraphs. Too often we focus on how students decode words – as in the ongoing phonics versus whole-language debate. But in that debate we neglect the importance of reading comprehension. A student may be able to "read" every word on a page and yet not understand what the text actually means.

I used to be an elementary-school teacher, so I remember doing running records with my students to assess their reading levels. It wasn't long before I noticed that my students performed much better on the comprehension questions after reading an article about a sports game than after reading an article about Dr. Norman Bethune, a Canadian physician who went to China in the early 20th century, even though both articles were officially at the same reading level. Why?

The problem with reading levels is that they focus on quantitative factors such as word complexity and sentence length, but fail to account for the important connection between specific content knowledge and reading comprehension. A student may be able to decode every single word in an article about Bethune, but still be clueless about the article's meaning since they know virtually nothing about communism, the Second Sino-Japanese War or blood transfusions.

In contrast, most students will breeze through an article about a hockey game because they know how the game works. They have no difficulty understanding phrases like high-sticking, pulling the goalie, and killing a penalty. However, imagine how hard it would be for someone who had never heard of hockey to understand an article that used these phrases. Prior knowledge about the game is actually more important to reading comprehension than the length and complexity of the words and sentences in the article.

Reading levels by themselves do a very poor job of matching students with the proper books to read. That was the finding of a peer-reviewed research study printed in the April 2018 edition of the journal *Reading and Writing.* James W. Cunningham, Elfrieda H. Hiebert, and Heidi Anne Mesmer examined two of the most widely used reading-level classification systems, the Lexile framework and the Flesch-Kincaid grade-level formula. Both systems have the aura of precision because it's relatively easy to calculate the average number of syllables in words, mean sentence length, and word frequencies. However, precision doesn't guarantee validity, particularly when it comes to reading comprehension. Cunningham, Hiebert, and Mesmer, in fact, found that "these two text tools may lack adequate validity for their current uses in educational settings."

By placing reading-level stickers on their classroom library books, teachers may be inadvertently preventing students from reading the books that would benefit them the most. Students who know a lot about a particular topic can read almost any book about it, no matter its assigned reading level. Conversely, students who know little about a topic will struggle with books at even the simplest reading levels.

This means schools must place much stronger emphasis on the acquisition of subject-specific content knowledge, particularly in the early grades when students are building up their general knowledge base. Instead of spending hours working on generic reading comprehension strategies, students should learn as many facts as possible about science, history, and today's world. Time spent classifying books into reading levels would be much better spent building up students' background knowledge.

The more knowledge students acquire, the more they will be able to learn. This is how we can help our students become stronger readers and gain a better understanding of our world.

GOOD TEACHERS KNOW THEIR SUBJECT MATTER

"TEACHERS – DON'T WORRY if you don't have the knowledge or skill set. You are the lead learner. Inquire not lecture."

This was an actual tweet from a prominent education guru. Sadly, this message is far from isolated. There is a common belief in education circles that teacher subject-matter expertise does not matter a whole lot.

The underlying assumption is that learning is more about a generalized process than it is about mastering subject-specific content. In other words, the journey matters more than the actual destination. Since knowledge changes so quickly, students should learn how to learn rather than spend their valuable time memorizing facts that will soon be outdated.

This thinking has been popularized by the 21st century skills movement. Advocates of this approach suggest that students need to work on generic skills such as creativity, cooperation, and critical thinking. Since these skills are allegedly transferable between different subjects, they will never become obsolete. This is why Canadian provinces such as Alberta and British Columbia are going through a curriculum revision process that involves reducing the amount of content in core subjects.

Look again at the tweet quoted earlier. It tells teachers not to worry if they do not have the knowledge or the skill set. It reminds them that they are lead learners and encourages them to inquire rather than to lecture. This is exactly the message you would expect from someone who does not value teacher expertise.

By this reasoning, it does not matter if math teachers know little about math. In fact, teachers who lack math knowledge or the specific skills to solve math problems may actually be more effective in the classroom, since they can learn the material together with their students. That is the message teachers often hear from the many gurus who speak at their professional development conferences.

Of course, no other profession would tolerate this kind of direct attack on expertise. Imagine telling a heart surgeon not to worry if she does not have the knowledge or skill set to perform heart surgery. Even more absurd would be telling airplane pilots that they don't need to know how to fly a plane because they can learn alongside their passengers. The reason we call people professionals is that they have specific expertise that the public lacks.

When it comes to teaching, there is a wealth of research that backs up the claim that teacher expertise matters, and it matters a lot. While some gurus apparently believe that one teacher is as good as another, the evidence is clear that some teachers are far more effective than others. Students fortunate enough to have a series of effective teachers experience significant academic benefits.

A 2018 study also validates the claim that the subject-specific knowledge of teachers, in fact, makes a noticeable difference to student achievement. The study, "Pulling Back the Curtain: Revealing the Cumulative Importance of High-Performing, Highly Qualified Teachers on Students' Educational Outcome," appeared in the journal *Educational Evaluation and Policy Analysis.* In it, Dr. Se Woong Lee analyzed a longitudinal data set involving more than 6000 students and their teachers across the US.

Dr. Lee found that students taught by math teachers who majored or even minored in mathematics at university had better short-term academic results than students taught by math teachers without a math major or minor. Not only that, but these students also benefited in the long-term, as they were more likely to graduate from college. If subject-matter expertise matters in math, it is reasonable to assume it matters in other subjects as well.

This is why it makes sense for teachers to teach subjects in which they are competent, completing at least a minor in their university studies. Teachers who know a lot about Canadian history are going to be more effective at teaching Canadian history than teachers who need a copy of *Canadian History for Dummies* in order to keep up with their students. The same holds true for teachers of chcmistry, physics, and geography, and all other subjects.

Teachers are not interchangeable factory widgets who can be replaced at the drop of a hat. Just as pilots are not merely lead fliers, teachers are much more than lead learners – they are, in fact, professionals who possess specialized knowledge and skills. Thus, teacher expertise really does matter. It benefits no one when education gurus downplay teacher expertise by saying that knowledge and skills do not matter.

~ 5 ~

DISCOVERY MATH DOESN'T ADD UP

BRIDGE 9340 OPENED in 1967 and was the US state of Minnesota's third-busiest bridge, carrying 140,000 vehicles daily. Forty years later, the bridge collapsed without warning during the evening rush hour. Thirteen people died. An investigation by the National Transportation Safety Board determined that the collapse was the result of a math error made by the engineers who designed the bridge.

Apparently, the designers failed to do some important calculations regarding the impact of the bridge's intended load on the steel-beam gusset plates. Had they done these calculations, they would have seen that the gusset plates were undersized and inadequate for the task. This error of omission resulted in lives being lost.

When it comes to designing a bridge, there is little room for error. Every calculation must be performed correctly. Make one mistake and the whole thing might collapse, as happened with Bridge 9340. This is a good reminder for progressive educators who insist that there is no need to focus on accuracy and speed in math classes.

This chapter's title is deliberately chosen because discovery math really doesn't add up. Instead of helping students to memorize the times tables, master their math facts, and learn the standard algorithms, discovery math focuses on getting students to develop their own strategies for solving math problems. The correct answer is seen as less important than the process of reaching a solution.

The *Math Makes Sense* textbook series – a misnomer if there ever was one – is a prime example of this confusing approach. Not only does it omit the standard algorithms for addition, subtraction, multiplication, and division, but it also shows students convoluted and confusing ways of solving even the simplest problems. The only math that makes sense in this textbook is the money the publisher makes when school boards purchase copies for their schools, which unfortunately is happening across North America.

The articles in this chapter chronicle the rise of discovery math in several Canadian provinces and the limited success that parent advocates and university math professors have had in fighting against this approach. One piece describes my personal encounter with one of the foremost proponents of discovery math at a parent meeting in Winnipeg. Suffice it to say, she had great difficulty defending her ideas to a skeptical audience of parents and informed teachers.

Discovery math is yet another example of the failed progressive education ideology. It may go by other names, such as inquiry learning or problem-based learning, but the impact remains the same: students end up confused and frustrated.

SASKATCHEWAN MATH CURRICULUM DOESN'T MAKE SENSE

FIVE TIMES FIVE equals 25. You may already know that, but many Saskatchewan students need a calculator to figure it out. That's because the new math curriculum in the province does not require students to memorize their multiplication tables. Also missing are the standard algorithms for addition, subtraction, multiplication, and division.

Instead, the curriculum encourages students to construct their own ways of doing math. As a result, students spend hours working on open-ended word problems with no obvious solution. When faced with basic arithmetic, elementary students regularly pull out their calculators.

Current math textbooks reflect this bias against traditional knowledge and skills. A prime example is Pearson Education's *Math Makes Sense*, a textbook series used in a variety of grade levels across Saskatchewan. As many parents and students can attest, the name of the series is a misnomer. The math in the textbooks doesn't make sense and simple problems are presented in confusing and convoluted ways.

In 2011, a group of math professors from Saskatchewan and Manitoba decided to take action. They formed an organization called the Western Initiative for Strengthening Education in Math (WISE Math). Largely in response to WISE Math, Saskatchewan's education minister, Donna Harpauer, organized a series of consultation meetings across the province with the intent of improving math education in schools. This initiative gave mathematicians hope that things would change for the better.

That hope faded when the education department issued a news release informing the public that it intended to make no changes to the math curriculum. Instead, Harpauer announced that teachers would be provided with more professional development opportunities to help them implement the new curriculum more effectively. The minister also encouraged schools to hold more information sessions for parents about the curriculum.

Of course, Harpauer's directives make about as much sense as holding professional development sessions about the unsinkability of the Titanic immediately after it hit the iceberg. Like the doomed Titanic, the math curriculum sinks under its own weight, and providing more information about it will not be of much help to students or their parents. The problem is a faulty curriculum, not a lack of information about its contents.

Harpauer defends her directives by arguing that Saskatchewan only began to implement this curriculum in 2007 and has not had sufficient time to evaluate its effectiveness. However, the philosophy behind the new curriculum is not really new at all.

Many math textbooks published in the 1990s and used across Western Canada already reflected elements of the "new math" approach. For example, Addison-Wesley's *Quest 2000* series of textbooks contained virtually no standard algorithms and encouraged students to use calculators to answer simple arithmetic questions. Like Saskatchewan's math curriculum, students spent much of their time on convoluted word problems, rather than on straightforward math questions.

Thus, the new curriculum simply formalized a long-standing shift away from traditional methods of teaching math. Prospective teachers were already being indoctrinated by education professors who disparaged any form of drill and practice. As a result, many schools had implemented elements of the new curriculum long before the most recent iteration was published in 2007. Despite what Harpauer says, there has been plenty of time to evaluate this approach.

In the background information provided with the news release, Harpauer emphasized that Saskatchewan has essentially the same math curriculum as other provinces in Western Canada. The implication is that it is pointless to question the new curriculum when it is already used in many other jurisdictions.

But the questions should not stop. Education has a long history of failed fads that once received universal praise. Saskatchewan's education minister needs to look past the edu-babble produced by her department and seriously consider how to make meaningful changes to the math curriculum.

This article was originally published in 2012

HOW TO MAKE MATH
EDUCATION WORSE
IN NOVA SCOTIA

PARENTS HAVE GOOD reason to be concerned about the state of math education in Nova Scotia. According to the Pan Canadian Assessment Program, Nova Scotia students score significantly below the Canadian average in mathematics.

Earlier in 2012, the Nova Scotia government pledged to improve math instruction by adopting the Alberta math curriculum. Presumably this means the purchase of new textbooks and lots of professional development seminars for teachers. Many of these training sessions will likely be coordinated by the Mathematics Teachers Association, an affiliate of the Nova Scotia Teachers Union.

However, the cure may be worse than the disease. Consider the decision of the Mathematics Teachers Association to have Dr. Marian Small give the keynote address at its upcoming conference (in October 2012). Dr. Small is the former dean of education at the University of New Brunswick and one of the foremost proponents in Canada of the "new math" approach. We can only assume that the Mathematics Teachers Association shares her perspective, since it chose her as its keynote speaker.

Math Focus, the textbook series authored by Dr. Small, reflects her random, abstract approach. For example, the standard algorithms for arithmetic, such as long division and vertical addition with a carry, are almost entirely absent. In their place, we find convoluted word problems, confusing instructions, and complicated diagrams. No wonder many parents find it difficult to help their kids with their math homework.

Recently, I had the opportunity to hear Dr. Small for myself. In September 2012, she gave an evening presentation to approximately 80 parents at an elementary school in Winnipeg, Manitoba. Because of her prominence in the field of math education, I assumed she would be able to make an intelligent case for her position. I was wrong.

During her presentation, Dr. Small emphasized that there was more than one way to get the correct answer, and encouraged teachers to assign more open-ended and ambiguous math questions to their students. Thus, she argued, all students would be more likely to get a correct answer on their questions. She added that all ways of solving math problems were equally valid and teachers should not make a student feel bad for using a different method.

At this point, I put up my hand and asked Dr. Small whether she felt teachers should include the standard algorithms as a component of math instruction. She replied that she did not. When I asked how she reconciled this with her earlier statement that all ways of solving math questions were equally valid, she insisted that the new math techniques were still better. The message I took from that exchange was that all methods were equally valid unless she didn't personally agree with them.

I wasn't the only audience member frustrated by the obvious logical inconsistencies in her presentation. Several math professors in the audience challenged some of Dr. Small's claims about math instruction. At this point, Dr. Small shut down the questions and said that she was simply going to proceed with her presentation. It was ironic that Dr. Small emphasized the importance of acknowledging the validity of other perspectives, but did exactly the opposite with her own presentation. She gave a one-sided lecture and refused to seriously engage with anyone who expressed an opposing view.

As for the much-vaunted decision of Nova Scotia's Department of Education to adopt the Alberta math curriculum, there is much less to this change than meets the eye. Alberta actually has the same math curriculum as the other provinces in Western Canada, as evidenced by their shared Western and Northern Canadian Protocol (WNCP). Throughout the implementation of this curriculum, Alberta's math test scores have declined.

The WNCP is heavily influenced by Dr. Small and her *Math Focus* textbook series is a recommended resource for teachers. But if the Nova Scotia government is serious about improving math instruction, it needs to move away from a nebulous, feel-good curriculum and adopt a rigorous curriculum that emphasizes the necessary knowledge and skills. Until then, we can expect math education in Nova Scotia to get worse.

BASIC MATH RETURNS
TO MANITOBA

FROM SEPTEMBER 2013, elementary students in Manitoba will have to memorize their times tables and solve basic equations without a calculator. They must also learn the standard algorithms for addition, subtraction, multiplication, and division.

After hearing this announcement, many parents were probably left with one question. Why were the math basics removed from the curriculum in the first place? How could anyone, for example, think it makes sense for students not to memorize their times tables?

The answer has everything to do with the philosophy behind the so-called "new math" approach. Advocates of this approach, also known as constructivism, say students need to construct their own ways of doing math. So instead of showing students the most efficient way of solving a question, teachers should give open-ended word problems to students and encourage them to invent their own problem-solving strategies.

One of the most prominent "new math" advocates is the math education professor Catherine Fosnot. You won't find students doing any multiplication drills at all if teachers follow her advice. But Fosnot is by no means the only math education professor to recommend the fact-free approach. In his widely distributed book series *Teaching Student-Centered Mathematics*, the late John Van de Walle disparages the teaching of standard algorithms. He also argues that skill-based drill and practice makes it harder for students to gain a deep conceptual understanding of mathematics.

Some math education professors go so far as to claim that teaching the standard algorithms to students is developmentally harmful. Constance Kamii, professor of early childhood education at the University of Alabama, co-authored a widely influential paper in

1998 entitled "The Harmful Effects of Algorithms in Grades 1–4." Even though the arguments contained in this paper have been thoroughly debunked by math professors, Kamii's dubious research is constantly cited by "new math" advocates.

The Western and Northern Canadian Protocol, which the Manitoba math curriculum is based upon, was strongly influenced by these education professors and their disciples. In addition, commonly used math textbooks such as the *Math Makes Sense* and *Math Focus* series are heavily infused with the "new math" approach – it is almost impossible to find any standard algorithms in either.

It took several years of concerted lobbying by parents, math professors, and other concerned citizens to get Manitoba to back away, ever so slightly, from the "new math" approach. The education minister finally saw the light and put basic skills back in the curriculum, but these changes did not come without a fight.

A letter in the *Winnipeg Free Press* shows just how entrenched the ideas behind "new math" have become among many educators. Neil Dempsey, a math support teacher, wrote that he was "dismayed by the backward step taken by the provincial government." Dempsey also bemoaned the move to "bring back the long division algorithm" and argued that other countries were moving away "from memorization of math facts." Far from representing a fringe perspective, Dempsey actually reflects the view of most math education professors and curriculum consultants.

So, although we should celebrate the return of basic skills to the Manitoba math curriculum, parents and other concerned citizens must remain vigilant. Many in the educational establishment would like nothing more than to put things back to how they were before.

NEW WAYS OF TEACHING
MATH DON'T PASS THE TEST

IN ALBERTA, WHEN it comes to math education, an unstoppable force has met an immovable object. On one side, we have the unstoppable Dr. Nhung Tran-Davies, backed up by thousands of equally frustrated parents. On the other, we have the immovable education minister, Jeff Johnson, supported by dozens of curriculum consultants and education professors who have staked their careers on discovery/inquiry math.

Tran-Davies is unstoppable because she has two key things on her side: public opinion and research evidence. Her petition calling on the Alberta government to restore conventional algorithms and the memorization of math facts to the curriculum has garnered more than 13,000 signatures, with more people signing up every day. In contrast, a counter-petition supporting discovery/inquiry math received a paltry 400 signatures.

In addition, more than 200 parents, students and real mathematicians (not math ed types) recently converged at a rally to demand the basics be restored. Parents across the province are fed up with fuzzy math textbooks and unproven techniques, and will no longer tolerate the education minister's fuzzy answers to their serious concerns.

Even more importantly, Tran-Davies is supported in her position by considerable research evidence. Her call for the direct teaching of standard algorithms and the memorization of basic math facts recognizes that students cannot progress to higher-level thinking in math unless they first have a solid understanding of foundational skills and concepts.

In their book *Visible Learning and the Science of How We Learn* (2014), which gives a summary of the empirical research evidence, the education researcher John Hattie and the cognitive psychologist Gregory Yates note that students who do not know their basic math facts invariably struggle when they progress to higher levels of math. In other words, using various strategies to solve 5 x 6 is a waste of mental energy since students should know automatically that the answer is 30. They should have memorized this in elementary school.

"There was a period in which teachers were encouraged to believe that rote learning stood in antagonism to deeper understanding. This notion is misleading since all indices of knowledge display positive associations … Repetition and consolidation are vehicles enabling knowledge to be stored within retrievable units, thereby accelerating mental growth through conceptual mastery and deeper understanding," conclude Hattie and Yates.

In contrast, the Alberta initiative, Inspiring Education, has little empirical support. Its underlying philosophy goes by various names (inquiry-based learning, discovery learning, constructivism), but the key idea in math is that students should develop their own problem-solving strategies. The widely used textbook series *Math Makes Sense* exemplifies this approach by asking students to figure out multiple ways of solving even the simplest of questions.

Despite its popularity among education department officials, many researchers have thoroughly debunked this approach. For example, in 2006, the journal *Educational Psychologist* published a study by the education researchers Paul Kirschner, John Sweller, and Richard Clark entitled "Why Minimal Guidance During Instruction Does Not Work: An Analysis of the Failure of Constructivist, Discovery, Problem-Based, Experiential, and Inquiry-Based Teaching."

The title of their article says it all. Kirschner, Sweller, and Clark showed that constructivist methodologies were considerably less effective than traditional methodologies. They concluded that "minimally guided instruction is less effective and less efficient than instructional approaches that place a strong emphasis on guidance of the student learning process." Since the Inspiring Education initiative is based on constructivist philosophy, there is good reason to question its effectiveness.

Unfortunately, Johnson has remained impervious to the concerns of parents and ignored the compelling research evidence. Although he recently conceded that students should memorize the multiplication tables, he still won't commit to putting standard algorithms back in the math curriculum. Furthermore, constructivist math textbook series such as *Math Makes Sense* and *Math Focus* remain Alberta Education's recommended resources.

Considering that Johnson was co-chair of the original steering committee for Inspiring Education, it isn't surprising that he remains wedded to the constructivist methodology. However, there comes a time when one must set aside personal preferences and acknowledge that the evidence points in a different direction. Now is the time for him to do this.

The battle between the unstoppable force, Tran-Davies, and the immovable object, Johnson, cannot go on forever. Johnson needs to climb down from his pedestal and acknowledge that Inspiring Education is lacking in both public support and research evidence. In this clash, for the good of Alberta students and their parents, the immovable object needs to move.

This article was originally published in 2014

SUBTRACTING NEW MATH IN SASKATCHEWAN

FINALLY, AFTER ENDURING years of fuzzy math, parents in Saskatchewan may have cause for hope. Not only did the provincial government's latest throne speech acknowledge that Saskatchewan students have the worst math skills in Canada, but it also pledged to address the problem with a "common-sense" plan focusing on the basics. That is, indeed, good news for parents and children in Saskatchewan.

During a recent radio interview, the newly minted education minister, Bronwyn Eyre, made it clear that she intended to change the way math is taught in Saskatchewan schools. Although Eyre is not the first education minister to bemoan the state of math scores, she is the first to propose a comprehensive set of reforms that would address the problem.

Among other things, Eyre expressed a willingness to implement cross-provincial numeracy assessments (also known as standardized testing), spoke favourably about a back-to-basics approach to math instruction, and acknowledged that the current approach to math teaching was driving parents and students "crazy." Eyre even suggested that students should have the right to a math textbook that actually shows them how to solve math problems step by step.

These statements are music to the ears of parents who are fed up with the nonsensical math assignments brought home by their children. When parents who work as accountants, engineers, or even university math professors have difficulty deciphering the convoluted word problems in textbooks such as *Math Makes Sense*, something is clearly amiss.

As these and many other frustrated parents already know, students need to master the basics in order to be successful in math. This means learning the standard algorithms for addition, subtraction, multiplication, and division, and memorizing facts such as the times tables. Mastery of the basics provides students with the foundational skills necessary to tackle more advanced math problems.

However, if Saskatchewan's education minister intends to introduce a common-sense approach to math instruction to schools, she will encounter heavy resistance from education professors and curriculum consultants. This resistance greets every minister who challenges the educational establishment.

The progressive education ideology, which de-emphasizes subject-specific content knowledge (such as learning the times tables) and encourages teachers to avoid direct instruction (actual teaching), now dominates the education system. Many math education professors (not to be confused with actual mathematicians) have built their entire careers on progressive ideology and will defend it vigorously, even in the face of contrary evidence.

As a case in point, Dr. Jo Boaler, a math education professor at Stanford University, is a regular speaker at teacher professional development conferences in Canada and the US. Boaler's ideas are about as far away from Eyre's proposed reforms as it is possible to get. In particular, Boaler stridently opposes the use of timed math drills and discourages students from using the standard algorithms. Sadly, she is only one of countless math education professors who promote this failed ideology.

Many grassroots teachers recognize the need for students to master the basics, but the same cannot be said for the hundreds of math consultants who work for education departments and school boards. Many of them are devoted disciples of math education professors like Boaler. For example, Jennifer Brokofsky, math coordinator for Saskatoon Public Schools, described Boaler as her "math hero" in an article she wrote for the Saskatchewan Mathematics Teachers' Society. Thus, it is highly unlikely that Brokofsky and other like-minded education consultants are going to welcome Eyre's new direction.

Eyre can also expect fierce resistance from within her own department. Many of the people working in the Saskatchewan education department come from the ranks of education superintendents and curriculum consultants, most of whom have climbed the career ladder by espousing progressive education ideas and enacting progressive policies. Eyre's department officials may not openly oppose her planned reforms, at least not to her face, but they won't exactly help her either. Watch the British political satire *Yes Minister* to see what this passive resistance might look like.

Saskatchewan has an opportunity to make substantial reforms to math instruction. Hopefully, Eyre overcomes resistance from the establishment and pushes ahead with her improvements.

This article was originally published in 2017

COMMON SENSE

« 6 »

PROPER GRADING AND REPORTING

YOU MIGHT REMEMBER Lynden Dorval. He was the public high school teacher in Edmonton, Alberta, who was fired in 2012 because he refused to follow his school's no-zero policy. Dorval could not abide by a policy that prohibited him from holding his students accountable when they didn't submit their work or submitted it late. His firing set off a storm of controversy, drawing attention to no-zero policies around the world. For a while he was the most famous, or infamous, teacher in North America.

In the end, Dorval was completely vindicated. Not only did the Alberta Board of Reference rule in his favour, but this decision was upheld by the Alberta Court of Appeal. In other words, Dorval's employer did not have adequate justification for firing him. Merely opposing his school's no-zero policy should not have cost him his job, but it did.

No-zero policies are the tip of the iceberg when it comes to the misguided approach of assessment gurus such as Damian Cooper and Ken O'Connor. These gurus insist on a rigid separation between academic achievement and behaviour on report cards – this leads to nonsensical no-zero policies, since the time at which an assignment is submitted is technically a behaviour. So entrenched are Cooper and O'Connor in this approach that they don't even think students should receive an academic penalty for plagiarism. Instead, plagiarists should simply be made to redo the assignment. It's kind of like telling a lawyer that if he gets caught suborning perjury, he'll just have to redo his examination of the witness.

The articles in this chapter tackle the topic of grading and reporting grades, and make the case for giving teachers much broader professional discretion. Not only should teachers decide on the appropriate grades for students, but they also should be allowed to write their own comments on report cards. In a number of jurisdictions, teachers are being forced to write "outcomes-based" comments that address behaviours such as study habits or homework completion. This is part of the philosophy that insists on a rigid separation between behaviour and academic work.

Several articles in this chapter deal with report cards and argue that a single percentage grade provides better information to students and parents than a long list of outcomes-based descriptors. Because percentage grades are readily understood by parents, schools should not rush to replace them with grades that are more difficult to understand. Ultimately, grades are about communication, and parents have a right to receive report cards that make sense to them.

DON'T ELIMINATE PERCENTAGE GRADES FROM REPORT CARDS

PARENTS CONCERNED ABOUT declining academic standards in public schools have another reason to worry. Traditional percentage grades may soon be a thing of the past if provincial officials and school division administrators have their way.

There are a number of reasons why school divisions choose to go in this direction. One of these is the belief among some education gurus that percentage grades are not an "authentic" form of assessment. They assert that since provincial curricula are designed according to targeted learning outcomes, a single percentage grade does not accurately inform parents and students about progress in relation to these outcomes. As a result, there is a need to design a new system for assessing achievement and reporting results.

In place of percentage grades is a four-point scale with descriptors for each learning outcome, such as: 1. Not yet meeting outcomes, 2. Meeting outcomes with assistance, 3. Meeting outcomes, and 4. Exceeding outcomes. On their report cards, instead of a single percentage grade by each subject, students see a long list of 1s, 2s, 3s, or 4s accompanied by learning outcome descriptors.

Not surprisingly, many students and parents have difficulty comprehending these report cards. Teachers and parents also find it hard to encourage students to improve their grades by a specific amount. For example, in schools with this scheme, parents cannot even assure their children that their grades will improve if they work a little harder, since so few achievement levels are measured.

A common response from those who support this assessment method is that parents oppose this system because they are not sufficiently informed. This response is an insult to the many parents who desire the best for their children and whose common sense tells them that removing percentage grades from report cards leads to a loss of precision in the reporting process. The problem is that too many education gurus who push this assessment methodology are divorced from the real world.

Another reason given for eliminating percentage grades is the need to protect the self-esteem of students. Education gurus claim that giving a mark of 25% to students damages their self-esteem and makes it harder for them to think they are capable of better. However, the reality is that failure is part of life and learning how to deal with it is an important part of everyone's development. Besides, it does not take long before students figure out that a list of 1s on the new report cards is the approximate equivalent of 25% on a regular report card.

Supporters of the new system are quick to claim that "all the research" proves percentage grades are an inferior form of reporting progress to parents. This is simply not true. There are many different types of education research, but much of it is highly subjective and anecdotal. Of course, there is systematic inquiry and research in education, but often the results are not strong enough to identify exactly what teachers should or should not do in their classrooms. Thus, school administrators cannot simply hide behind the research argument when implementing a new report card system.

Parents need information on the achievement and progress of their children that is as accurate as possible, reasonably precise, and readily understandable. For this reason alone, they do not deserve the imprecise and confusing information that characterizes some report cards. Grades must communicate, not obfuscate, students' genuine degree of achievement and progress. Percentages are an easily understandable and accurate form of communicating achievement to students and parents, and should remain on report cards.

ASSIGNMENT DEADLINES SHOULD MATTER IN SCHOOL

MANITOBA TEACHERS MAY soon have the option again of deducting marks for late assignments. The education minister, Nancy Allan, has acknowledged that the directive that forbids teachers from using academic penalties for lateness is problematic. "Right now we have a one-size-fits-all policy that I don't believe is working," said Allan in a media interview.

That is an understatement. When students know they cannot be academically penalized for handing their assignments in late, many of them submit the work weeks past the deadline, if at all. Although teachers are encouraged to stress the importance of deadlines with their students, this policy prevents them from imposing any meaningful consequences.

It's akin to a newspaper publisher telling an editor to ensure that journalists submit their news stories on time, yet informing her that she cannot discipline employees who consistently file their stories late. Of course, any newspaper that operated in this manner would quickly go out of business. That's the difference between the real world and an education system removed from reality courtesy of fads and political directives.

Manitoba is not the only Canadian province to have this type of policy. Ontario has similar assessment guidelines, although that province does allow for the deduction of marks for lateness "as a last resort." However, because Ontario strongly recommends that teachers avoid penalizing lateness, its policy has become almost as rigid as Manitoba's.

In 2009, the Ottawa bargaining unit of the Ontario Secondary School Teachers' Federation surveyed its membership to gauge the practical impact of these guidelines. In total, 560 teachers responded to the survey, about a third of the bargaining unit's membership. Unsurprisingly, since the introduction of the no-late-penalty guidelines, 62% of teachers had seen a rise in student absenteeism and skipped tests. A whopping 84% had seen an increase in the number of late assignments. More than two-thirds of the teachers expressed dissatisfaction with the options available to them for dealing with late assignments.

One standard argument for current assessment policies is that they are backed up by solid research. "Overwhelming research shows that failing students or giving them zeros does not cause them to 'learn their lesson' and succeed in the long run," stated Kathleen Wynne, Ontario's education minister, earlier this year.

However, we should take these "overwhelming research" claims with a grain of salt. The history of public schooling in North America is littered with failed reforms, including open-area classrooms that looked great in the abstract but failed to work when implemented in real schools with real students. In another contrast between the imagined and real worlds, the nature of research in the social sciences is considerably "softer" than in the physical sciences. We would be well-advised to be skeptical of claims about "proof" provided by such malleable research.

The practical results of assessment policies that restrict the ability of teachers to penalize tardiness or give zeros for incomplete work are clear to see. Schools that implement these policies find that more students submit their work late, teacher workload and frustration increases, and opposition from parents and other concerned citizens mounts. If there is such an overwhelming body of research for the effectiveness of these practices, perhaps supporters of the policies could point us to some real-life schools where they have actually been successful.

Although Manitoba's education minister has not given a firm commitment to changing course, the fact that this directive is being reconsidered is a positive development. Let's hope this is the first step in the return of common sense to our public schools.

This article was originally published in 2010

SOMETIMES STUDENTS NEED TO GET A ZERO

HOW MUCH SHOULD a pilot get paid if she never flies a plane? How about a doctor who never treats a patient? Or a car salesman who fails to sell a single car?

If you answered zero, you live in the real world. Employees don't get paid for doing nothing. It's common sense.

However, some schools seem to have a different perspective. Many school administrators have introduced a grading-for-learning approach, part of which prohibits teachers from giving a mark of zero to students who submit incomplete assignments. Instead, teachers must assess students only on the work they actually hand in. In other words, students who don't complete many assignments can still pass their courses if they do well on the work they do submit.

Lynden Dorval teaches high school physics at Ross Sheppard High School in Edmonton, Alberta. He recently refused to comply with the school's absurd grading policy prohibiting teachers from giving zeros for incomplete work. Dorval, who has 35 years of experience, went on giving zeros despite several warnings from his principal. Eventually he was suspended and could very well lose his job.

PROPER GRADING AND REPORTING

From a legalistic perspective, the school board has every right to discipline Dorval. According to Alberta's School Act, boards may suspend teachers who fail to follow a lawful directive, even if the policy in question is misguided. Schools cannot function if teachers disregard any policy they disagree with.

That being said, most people recognize that there is something intuitively wrong with an assessment policy that prohibits teachers from assigning zeros for work that has not been done. The fact that many of Dorval's colleagues and students are rallying behind him should be a clear sign that something is seriously amiss. This is a policy that may be lawful, but that most members of the public consider illegitimate and indefensible.

Yet Edmonton's superintendent, Edgar Schmidt, has published an open letter defending the indefensible. He stands by the policy of not giving zeros and tries to present it as a superior way of holding students accountable. "Our approach to missed assignments is to work with each student to find out the reason they did not turn in an assignment. Once a teacher finds out the reason, they work with the student to come up with a solution to address the situation. They agree to a plan to turn in future assignments and the teacher holds the student accountable," Schmidt writes.

This explanation does not address the fact that some students simply choose not to do their work. Dorval didn't automatically give zeros to students the moment an assignment didn't arrive. Rather, he worked with students and reminded them regularly of the importance of submitting their work. When that fails, however, there needs to be a tangible consequence for those students who choose not to do the work. This assessment policy naively ignores the realities of human nature.

Ross Sheppard High School is by no means the first to experiment with this failed approach. Manitoba and Ontario had provincial assessment policies that prohibited or strongly discouraged teachers from deducting marks from late assignments or giving zeros for incomplete work. However, strong opposition from the public led both governments to retreat from this policy.

It never had to be this way. Many aspects of the so-called grading-for-learning approach are positive and would likely have broad-based public support. For example, grading for learning encourages teachers to drop the common practice of basing individual student assessment on group assignments. It also makes a clearer distinction between assignments given for the purpose of preliminary feedback (formative assessment) and final marks (summative assessment). These are sensible reforms, but they have been overshadowed by the no-zero policy.

School administrators have a choice. They can focus on common-sense assessment reforms that would have broad-based public support, or they can stand behind a foolish no-zero policy supported by a handful of education consultants.

This article was originally published in 2012

PERCENTAGES BELONG ON REPORT CARDS

SUPPOSE YOU HAVE two Grade 8 students in the same science class. We'll call them Ken and Damian. Ken received a mark of 85% on his report card, while Damian got 96%. Who did better in science?

For most people, this question is easy to answer. Although both students did well, Damian's higher mark indicates that he outperformed Ken. Damian probably received slightly better scores on his tests, submitted higher-quality assignments, and demonstrated a superior understanding of the subject matter. In other words, there is a real and measurable difference between a good student like Ken and an excellent student like Damian.

However, some school division officials apparently think Ken and Damian deserve the same mark. For example, Battle River School Division, based in Camrose, Alberta, requires its teachers to grade student work at one of four levels: beginning, developing, achieving, or excelling. Since the "excelling" level has a range of 84–100, both Ken and Damian would receive the same mark.

Unsurprisingly, the new grading system is not going over well with parents or students in Battle River. A recent rally at the school division's office attracted more than 150 students and parents, while about 2,800 parents and 300 students have signed a petition opposing the system. Despite the resistance, the school division has given no indication that it plans to change course.

The philosophy underpinning the new approach is known as outcomes-based assessment. Essentially, it states that students should be evaluated based on how well they master specific learning targets, known as outcomes. For example, an outcome for a Grade 5 math course might be "use two-digit multiplication to solve real-life math problems." The teacher would then give a mark based on how well a student achieves that particular outcome.

So far, there is nothing particularly objectionable about this approach. After all, it makes sense to specify what skills students need to master in each subject. It also is reasonable for teachers to use a four-point scale to evaluate some types of student work based on these learning outcomes. Problems arise when school administrators toss aside common sense and impose rigid assessment policies that lead to unnecessary conflicts with parents and students. Sometimes policies that sound good in theory do not translate well into the real classroom setting.

The no-zero policy at Ross Sheppard High School in Edmonton, which led to the firing of the physics teacher Lynden Dorval, is a case in point. Ross Sheppard's then-principal followed outcomes-based assessment to the letter when he instructed teachers not to give zeros for missing work. This was based on the conviction that grades must only reflect the achievement of learning outcomes. Of course, Ross Sheppard teachers found out very quickly that many students do not submit their work on time – or at all – if there is no academic penalty for lateness. No-zero policies may sound good to ivory tower academics, but they don't work in real classrooms.

The removal of percentage grades from report cards is another example of this disconnect between assessment theory and classroom reality. While it may make sense to grade some assignments on a four-point scale, there is no need to extend this to every assignment. Some assignments are more complex than others and have many possible proficiency levels. Percentage grades make it possible to differentiate between good work and excellent work in a way that simply cannot be done when teachers are limited to four achievement levels.

In addition, most students still write unit tests where even more levels of proficiency are possible. A student who answers all 50 math questions correctly on a test should receive a higher grade than another student who answers 44 questions correctly. Conversely, it is much worse to answer only three questions correctly than 24, yet both these students would receive the same "beginning" grade under the Battle River system.

It is also important to recognize that percentage grades are a form of communication that virtually all parents understand. Even if strict adherence to the principles of outcomes-based assessment was technically correct, school divisions need to weigh this against the need to work with parents and provide them with comprehensible information about student achievement. Administrators who wish to overhaul grading practices need to ask themselves whether the change they seek is so important that it necessitates alienating a large number of parents and students.

In this latest clash between theory and reality in public education, let's hope reality wins for a change. Percentages belong in classrooms and on report cards.

This article was originally published in 2013

NEW REPORT CARDS ARE
A LESSON IN FAILURE

IT IS SOON going to be a lot more difficult for parents in Calgary, Alberta, to figure out how their kids are doing in school. Instead of standard letter or percentage grades, parents can look forward to finding out whether their kids are in the "exemplary," "evident," "emerging," or "support required" categories.

As a part of a pilot project in a number of its schools, the Calgary Board of Education is introducing new report cards. Not only will there be no letter or percentage grades, but teachers will no longer provide written comments. In addition, report cards will be sent home only twice a year instead of three or four times. Eventually, the board intends to implement the new report cards from kindergarten to Grade 9.

Advocates of this approach claim it will improve communication with parents. However, only someone immersed in edu-babble could seriously believe that replacing well-known letter grades and percentages with vague descriptors makes it easier for parents to understand how their kids are doing. For most parents, the difference between traditional grades such as a B and a D is a lot more obvious than the difference between "evident" and "emerging."

Unfortunately, parents had better work at deciphering the "evident" and "emerging" descriptors, since they are likely to appear most frequently on report cards. This is because "exemplary" means a student is performing well above grade level – usually only a small percentage of students in any class. After all, if most students in a grade consistently perform above grade level, then the skills being evaluated will likely be moved to a different grade level.

As for the "support required" descriptor, this is a new code word for failure. However, since we all know that failure is almost impossible at the elementary levels, it is reasonable to assume those parents will rarely see "support required" on report cards. There may be some interesting conversations at home when parents try to encourage their kids to be more "evident" in their two-digit multiplication skills.

To make matters even more confusing, the new report cards will not contain any personalized comments from teachers. The school board says these comments are unnecessary because teachers will communicate more regularly with parents, but the fact remains that written comments on report cards are a prime opportunity for teachers to provide important information to parents, particularly those with younger children. The removal of personalized comments from report cards may lighten the workload of teachers, but it won't benefit students or parents.

Advocates of these kinds of reporting systems frequently claim they have research evidence on their side. This claim is patently false. There is no body of research showing that the removal of percentage or letter grades in public schools leads to improved student achievement. While it is true that some students and parents prefer nebulous or non-existent grades, it is equally true that many students and parents prefer a rigorous grading system that enables them to track their academic progress.

What research does show is that timely and understandable feedback from teachers to students and parents is extremely important. Traditional letter and percentage grades are far from perfect, but they are a long-standing and necessary form of feedback. They should not be abandoned without very good reason.

This article was originally published in 2013

A VICTORY FOR COMMON SENSE IN SCHOOLS

REMEMBER LYNDEN DORVAL? He's the Edmonton teacher who made national news in 2012 when he was fired by his school division for defying his principal's no-zero edict. Many of his colleagues, parents, and students stood with him.

Public opinion was overwhelmingly on Dorval's side. Few people could see the logic in a policy that prohibited teachers from giving zeros for work that was never handed in. However, that didn't stop no-zero advocates from claiming that research supported their position. My own research report, *Zero Support for No-Zero Policies*, which came out in 2012, found that the exact opposite was true. No-zero policies are built on a house of sand.

I knew the evidence for the no-zero approach was weak before writing the report, but even I was surprised at just how flimsy the case for it really was. No-zero supporters make grandiose claims, then quote each other as "experts" to buttress their position. When these gurus do cite an actual research report, it doesn't even show what they claim it does.

Perhaps the most egregious example is the way in which assessment gurus like Ken O'Connor regularly claim that zeros cause students to withdraw from learning. However, the only research study ever cited to back up this claim looked at six students with learning disabilities in one British Columbia classroom more than 20 years ago. It is obviously absurd to project the experiences of six students on to the entire student population, but that is exactly what no-zero advocates do when they cite this study again and again.

When Dorval was dismissed from his job, he filed an appeal with the Alberta Board of Reference. As a tenured teacher, Dorval was entitled to have an independent panel review his case and determine whether the school division had sufficient cause for dismissal. The board found that Edmonton Public Schools had acted improperly when it fired Dorval.

According to the *Edmonton Journal*, "the board said there was no evidence Dorval was deliberately disobeying lawful instructions. He wasn't given a full opportunity to fight the allegations against him or ask questions during his dismissal hearing in September 2012." In other words, school administrators failed to follow proper procedure.

Even more revealing was the way in which the board criticized the implementation of the no-zero policy itself. In its ruling, the board noted that the policy had a negative impact on student motivation. Since there was no academic penalty for incomplete assignments, there was little incentive for students to finish them. In addition, the policy was imposed on teachers without any meaningful consultation.

The Board of Reference's decision could set an important precedent for Alberta teachers and perhaps even for teachers across Canada. Although teachers have a duty to follow lawful orders from their employers, those orders cannot be arbitrary or capricious. The board found that Dorval and other teachers at his school had legitimate concerns about the no-zero policy, but the principal did not adequately address them. In addition, two other teachers at Dorval's school also refused to follow the policy, yet only Dorval was dismissed.

A spokesperson for Edmonton Public Schools wasted little time announcing its intent to appeal this ruling. Considering the profound impact this ruling could have on the relationship between teachers and administrators, the case will be closely followed by many interested parties.

Dorval's courageous actions against a nonsensical policy inspired many teachers across the country. The decision by the Board of Reference shows that sometimes the good guys really do win.

LET TEACHERS USE THEIR JUDGMENT ON REPORT CARDS

NOVA SCOTIA'S EDUCATION minister, Karen Casey, has demonstrated achievement in some of the learning outcomes for this year. She recognizes that parents deserve to receive report cards that actually make sense. But she has not yet demonstrated the ability to significantly revise the onerous comment-writing guidelines and would benefit from using some common sense.

The above paragraph is an example of the mind-numbing drivel many teachers are still required to write on students' report cards. Instead of simply using their judgment to write an appropriate comment, teachers must follow a laborious set of comment-writing criteria at all grade levels.

For example, the Tri-County Regional School Board in rural Nova Scotia provides its teachers with a 15-page manual called *Creating Strong Report Card Comments*. Among other things, teachers are expected to identify at least one strength, challenge, and next step for each student in every subject area. Think this is easy? The manual also reminds teachers not to refer to any behaviours such as study habits, homework completion, attendance, or attitude in their comments. It even provides a list of "useful" descriptors such as "successfully interprets," "has not yet demonstrated understanding," and "needs more time to develop."

So, instead of telling parents that their kids would get better marks if they studied for tests, showed up for class, and finished their homework, teachers are forced to write excessively wordy comments. Each comment is also expected to relate to a specific learning outcome. Hence parents must decipher statements such as: "She could identify some cultural groups that have settled in, but struggled to explain their impact on, Canada. Student only occasionally used this learning to demonstrate an understanding of the interactions among people and places over time and the resulting effects on the environment. She needs to consider alternate points of view." This comment was taken verbatim from Tri-County's report card manual.

Much of this useless verbiage stems from requiring teachers to identify an outcome-specific strength in every subject, even when the student is doing poorly and obviously needs to put more effort into their work. Similarly, teachers must provide specific challenges and next steps for high-achieving students who just need to keep doing what they are doing. In these situations, old-fashioned comments such as "more effort required" or "excellent progress" would be a better way of getting the message across.

Commendably, the education minister acknowledged last year that report cards could not be understood by parents. She even ordered some sensible changes, such as including percentage marks on report cards for grades 7 and 8, and telling teachers to cut back on the impersonal, bureaucratic language. However, her department's press release announcing these changes still mentions the strengths, challenges, and next steps that teachers are expected to include in every comment. For the most part, the same onerous and convoluted comment-writing guidelines must be followed.

Forcing teachers to include strengths, challenges, and next steps in every comment without making reference to behaviour has more to do with enforcing a particular assessment ideology than improving student achievement. In the end, no one benefits – except the consultants who get paid to try to solve the problems they themselves created.

Things would work a lot better if teachers could just write whatever comments they think are appropriate on report cards. After all, they have five or more years of university education – they should know how to write reasonable and relevant comments on their own. In the area of assessment, teachers need more professional autonomy, not less.

In this case, the next step for the education minister is obvious. She needs to reject her department's rigid assessment ideology and empower teachers to use their own judgment on report cards.

This article was originally published in 2015

NO-ZERO POLICY FINALLY GETS A FAILING GRADE

THE LONG-STANDING NO-ZERO policy in Newfoundland and Labrador schools is no more. The chief executive officer of the province's English School District has announced that teachers are once again free to deduct marks for late work and assign zeros when work doesn't arrive at all.

This is a significant step forward, not only because no-zero policies have proven to be ineffective, but because the school district has long refused to acknowledge that it had one in place. As recently as 2015, the previous CEO, Darrin Pike, told the media that the English School District did not have a no-zero approach. Teachers knew better, of course. That's the reason the Newfoundland and Labrador Teachers' Association never relented in its demand to revoke this misguided policy.

No-zero policies are the brainchild of assessment gurus like Ken O'Connor and Damian Cooper, who argue that report cards should rigidly separate student behaviour from academic achievement. They maintain that because handing work in late, cheating on assignments, or not submitting an assignment are technically behaviours, these actions should not have an impact on a student's final mark in the course.

This might make sense in theory, but anyone who teaches in a real classroom with real students knows it almost never works. The moment students find out that they can hand in their assignments any time or not at all with no penalty, teacher deadlines become meaningless. Similarly, if the worst consequence for cheating is being required to redo the assignment, some students will take the risk. After all, they have nothing to lose.

To further illustrate the absurdity of no-zero policies, consider what happens in a class where students are expected to hand in ten assignments. Since teachers can't give zeros for work that doesn't come in, students quickly figure out they can choose the assignments they actually want to do. Of course, nowhere in the real world do things operate in such a ridiculous manner. Employees are required to complete all of their tasks, not just the ones they like to do. Fail to complete work and they will soon find themselves unemployed.

Now that the no-zero policy has finally been repealed, Newfoundland and Labrador educators should consider what lessons can be learned from this debacle. The first is that bad education policies have incredible staying power. Newfoundland and Labrador teachers laboured under the absurd no-zero policy for half a decade. It took years of lobbying from teachers and parents to get the English School District to see the light on this issue.

Second, the battle against a misguided policy needs to be waged on two fronts. It's important to provide solid reasons why a policy is mistaken. But the other front is getting a school district to acknowledge that a particular policy even exists. Although the no-zero policy was as plain as day to teachers, successive CEOs of the English School District continually denied that it existed, which made it difficult to lobby for its removal.

A third lesson is that evidence alone will not result in a policy change. Even when research studies exposed as a house of cards the claims made by assessment gurus, supporters of the no-zero approach remained unfazed. The policy is finally gone from Newfoundland and Labrador because teachers, parents, journalists, and politicians read the research evidence and spoke out, forcing the school district to make the right decision.

Finally, no-zero policies are merely the tip of the iceberg when it comes to misguided educational fads. From rigid inclusion to project-based discovery learning to differentiated instruction, Newfoundland and Labrador teachers are bombarded with bad ideas. Instead of trusting the professional judgment of teachers who read and understand the research literature, school and divisional administrators force them to adopt the latest fads.

Getting rid of the no-zero policy was a step in the right direction. However, there are a whole lot of other misguided educational policies that need to be axed. Let's hope the pressure continues and meaningful change happens.

~ 7 ~

IMPROVING LIFE FOR TEACHERS AND STUDENTS

"TAG! YOU'RE IT!" For most readers, this phrase probably brings back memories from elementary school. Tag is one of the simplest games ever devised. It requires no equipment, can be played at any age, and takes only seconds to learn. On top of that, it's a great way to get exercise, since participants spend most of their time running around. In many ways, tag is the perfect recess activity.

Incredibly, a number of schools in the US and the UK have banned tag during recess. They argue that the game is unsafe because students are constantly touching and bumping into each other. This violates their "hands off" policy, so students are redirected to non-contact games. Needless to say, these bans have not gone over well with parents, who find it frustrating when schools ban normal and active childhood games.

Sadly, this is far from the only nonsensical policy that schools have implemented. Several articles in this chapter describe schools that ban students from using soccer balls and skipping ropes during recess, require adult supervisors to stand near the microwaves where students heat up their lunches, and ban peanut butter substitutes from lunches because they look like peanut butter, which some students are allergic to. Although it is important to ensure safety at school, these draconian rules make life difficult for the students who have to follow them and the teachers who are required to enforce them.

At the opposite end of the spectrum are schools that err on the side of allowing student misbehaviour. Prominent edu-gurus such as Alfie Kohn argue that schools should be fully egalitarian communities without rewards and punishments for students. This permissive idealism fails to address the very real problem of misbehaviour and undermines teacher authority. Sadly, even though Kohn has no public school teaching experience, his ideas are widely promoted within North American schools.

The articles in this chapter cover a wide range of topics. Lengthening the school day, reducing class sizes, and recruiting more substitute teachers are a few examples. One of the pieces tackles the issue of how to deal with students who use social media to complain about their teachers. Clearly, today's teachers face challenges that would have been unimaginable just a generation ago.

Ultimately, the best way to improve life for everyone in a school is to set teachers free and let them teach. This is the theme of the final articles in this chapter. In 2013, the British teacher Tom Bennett held a professional development conference called researchED. It was unlike many other professional development conferences in that it welcomed a variety of perspectives and encouraged teachers to directly engage with and even challenge research findings. ResearchED conferences now take place around the world.

The age of the internet has made it possible for teachers to learn more than ever before about their profession. With grassroots organizations like researchED, teachers finally have a real opportunity to be heard by policymakers and parents.

CALLING TIME ON CELL PHONES IN SCHOOL

A LAWSUIT AGAINST a Saskatchewan school division threatens to undermine even more the ability of schools to establish a safe and orderly learning environment. The case directly pits the privacy rights of students against the right of administrators to maintain order in schools.

The circumstances behind this lawsuit began with a routine matter of discipline. A 12-year-old student was caught using his cell phone in a Prince Albert school where such devices are banned. The teacher confiscated the student's phone and handed it into the office.

Things became more complicated when the vice-principal discovered text messages on the phone about a recently stolen vehicle. Because of the illegal activity involved, the vice-principal contacted and handed the matter over to police. Upon meeting with the student, the police told him to send a text asking about the location of the vehicle. The police used the response to track down the stolen vehicle and then released the student.

The student's grandparents allege that the vice-principal violated their grandson's right to privacy when he looked at the text messages on the confiscated cell phone. They further allege that the actions of the police made it possible for criminals to identify their grandson as a police informant. As a result, they lived in fear of retaliation and drove their grandson out of Prince Albert every weekend to stay with relatives. Eventually, their grandson moved away to live with his mother on a permanent basis.

The grandparents are now suing the school division for CA$50,000 in punitive damages, along with an additional CA$1424 in travel costs. They allege that their grandson has anger problems and his grades have dropped as a result of this incident. In their view, all of their grandson's problems stem from the vice-principal looking at his cell phone.

Instead of affirming the importance of the teacher and vice-principal enforcing clear disciplinary policies, these grandparents sided with their grandson even though his actions were the direct cause of his predicament. Parents and guardians should not take school administrators to court simply because they disagree with the way rules are enforced.

As for this particular case, it's unrealistic for a 12-year-old student to have an expectation of privacy when using a device banned from the classroom. It is well established that teachers who confiscate notes passed from one student to another during class have every right to read those notes. Text messaging on cell phones has, in many ways, become the 21st-century version of note-passing. If there's something on your phone you don't want the teacher to see, don't use it in the classroom.

While it is true that section 8 of the Canadian Charter of Rights and Freedoms guarantees the right "to be secure against unreasonable search or seizure," the courts have also ruled that students in school cannot have the same expectation of privacy as the general public. For example, in a 1998 decision known as R. v. M. (M.R.), the Supreme Court of Canada ruled that a vice-principal who searched a 13-year-old student for drugs in the presence of a police officer did not violate that student's right to be secure against unreasonable search or seizure.

In that decision, Justice Peter Cory, writing for the majority, affirmed the importance of giving school administrators the authority to enforce school rules and maintain discipline and order. "School authorities must be accorded a reasonable degree of discretion and flexibility to enable them to ensure the safety of their students and to enforce school regulations," concluded Justice Cory.

As for the Prince Albert student's fear of retaliation from criminals, it seems patently obvious that his situation was entirely of his own making. He chose to bring a cell phone into class despite knowing it was banned and he chose to use that same phone to communicate with a car thief. Unfortunately, instead of encouraging their grandson to take responsibility for his decisions, the grandparents chose to blame the school system.

Teachers and school administrators face many challenges in trying to maintain order and discipline in our schools. Frivolous lawsuits like these are part of the problem.

This article was originally published in 2011

TAKING SAFETY
TO EXTREMES

SAFETY FIRST, COMMON sense last. That seems to be the motto when it comes to public schools. In 2011, the principal of Earl Beatty Public School in Toronto sent a letter to parents informing them that hard balls such as soccer balls, volleyballs, tennis balls, and footballs were now banned from school property. "Any balls brought will be confiscated and may be retrieved by parents from the office. The only kind of ball allowed will be nerf balls or sponge balls," explained the letter.

Although the Earl Beatty principal's decision was extreme, it is typical of the lack of common sense in public schools. Such an overarching emphasis on student safety makes little allowance for any activity that involves some level of risk and results in nonsensical decisions such as the one described above.

The trend toward safer but blander school playgrounds reflects an obsession with safety. Most adults today probably remember playing on the merry-go-round and teeter-totter when they attended school. Unfortunately, these devices have been removed from most playgrounds over concerns that they are dangerous. Swings, slides, and monkey bars have not been spared. Although they remain at some schools, they have been redesigned to be safer and more boring.

The exaggerated emphasis on safety has unhealthy consequences. A 2011 article by the psychologists Ellen Sandseter and Leif Kennair argues that experiencing moderate levels of risk and danger helps children overcome their natural fears. These psychologists suggest that we can expect "an increased neuroticism or psychopathology in society if children are hindered from partaking in age adequate risky play."

The focus on safety also affects what students may eat in school. Given the prevalence of peanut allergies among students, many schools have been declared "nut-free." Parents are told to make sure their children do not bring lunches that contain peanuts or peanut products. The life-threatening nature of some nut allergies makes this ban understandable and necessary.

However, the decision of a school board in London, Ontario, to ban peanut butter substitutes is simply ridiculous. Although it tastes exactly like peanut butter, WowButter is a product developed by Hilton Soy Foods that contains no peanuts. Nevertheless, the school board decided to ban WowButter because students and teachers might mistake it for real peanut butter.

It's one thing to ban peanut products from a school out of a desire to protect allergic students from exposure to peanuts. It's another thing entirely to ban a peanut-free product because it looks like peanut butter. This type of ban does nothing to make anyone safer and frustrates parents who simply want to provide healthy lunches for their children.

It would be nice if the situations I have described were merely isolated examples, but the overemphasis on safety can be found at schools right across North America. The Manitoba government has joined in: it has expanded the scope of the *Workplace Safety and Health Act* so that it now applies to all school divisions in the province. As a result, every school division must establish a workplace health and safety committee with representation from each of its employee groups. At least four health and safety inspections of each workplace must take place every year.

Along with their many other responsibilities, Manitoba school principals are now swamped in safety rules regulating everything from the proper placement of extension cords in classrooms to the use of microwaves during lunch. Apparently, students can no longer be trusted to do something as simple as heat up their own lunch in the microwave without an adult supervisor standing right next to them.

There seems to be no end to examples of safety silliness. When students aren't allowed to kick a soccer ball, play a game of tag, heat their lunch in the microwave, or use a skipping rope, we know that a safety-obsessed culture has gone off the rails. Safety is important, but so is common sense.

FINNISH LESSONS FOR CANADA

FINLAND MAY BE a tiny Northern European country with only 5.5 million people, but don't be fooled by its modest size and remote location. When it comes to student achievement, Finland punches well above its weight. In fact, Finnish students regularly outperform students from all around the world on international assessments of reading, writing, and science.

The Finnish education system has several key components. At its heart is the *peruskoulu*, a comprehensive nine-year municipal school where all students aged 7–16 follow the same basic educational program. Beyond that, upper secondary school is optional, although the vast majority of students choose to attend. They go on to an academic secondary school or a vocational secondary school until they complete the required credits for graduation.

In his book *Finnish Lessons: What Can the World Learn From Educational Change in Finland?* (2012), Pasi Sahlberg explains how Finland transformed its school system over several decades. As a native Finn and a former high-level official with the Finnish Ministry of Education and Culture, Sahlberg is well-positioned to describe the Finnish school system to the outside world.

He is not shy about identifying the factors that he believes have led to Finland's strong educational performance. The high quality of the country's teachers receives the most attention. In Finland, teaching is considered an esteemed profession that ranks right up there with medicine, law, and engineering. Only one out of every ten applicants is accepted to teacher training programs and all prospective teachers must complete a research-based master's degree.

Teachers are expected to have extensive knowledge of the subjects they teach. Primary school teachers must take a wide variety of subject-specific courses before completing their master's degree in education, while secondary teachers are expected to earn master's degrees in their subject area. Thus, a Finnish teacher who walks into his or her classroom is virtually guaranteed to be the most knowledgeable person in the room.

Despite their relatively low pay (only US$41,000 annually after 15 years of experience), teacher turnover is low and most teachers remain in the profession on a long-term basis. Teachers in Finland prioritize their working conditions and professional autonomy much more highly than their salaries.

Sahlberg also notes that Finland has avoided some of the education reforms most common in other countries. Most notably, Finland shuns standardized tests, does little to provide school choice to parents, and discourages competition between schools. Sahlberg believes these types of reforms are unnecessary and counter-productive. Unsurprisingly, education professors and teacher union officials latch on to these aspects of Finland's education system and propose we avoid standardized testing and school choice in Canada as well.

However, there are several flaws with this position. One of the most obvious is that Finland's education system would not even have been noticed by the rest of the world were it not for a standardized achievement test, the Programme for International

Student Assessment (PISA). PISA evaluates basic skills in reading, writing, mathematics, and science. International interest in Finland's education system only began when its students started showing substantial gains in student achievement, as measured by PISA. In other words, Finland's status as having one of the best education systems in the world rests entirely on the results from standardized achievement tests. If standardized testing is invalid, then there is no basis on which to claim the superiority of Finland's education system.

It's also not entirely accurate to say that Finland shuns standardized testing. The country requires all high school students in the academic stream to write a national matriculation examination. Sahlberg describes it as a "high stakes external examination" that has a "notable effect on curriculum and instruction." Since most Canadian provinces do not have an exit exam of this nature for their high school graduates, the Finland model is actually more rigorous in this regard.

As for competition and school choice, it should be noted that Finland is far more culturally homogeneous than Canada or the US. When most people come from the same cultural background and have similar socioeconomic status, the need for school choice is less urgent. However, in more diverse nations like ours, the best way to respect these differences is to allow parents greater say in the schools their children attend.

There is much we can learn from the Finnish school system. However, we need to be careful not to jump to hasty conclusions about what their experience means for us.

LONGER SCHOOL DAYS WILL NOT MAKE STUDENTS SMARTER

SUPPOSE A PROVINCIAL health minister announces that the best way to improve health care is to lengthen the average time each patient spends with his or her physician. Millions of dollars are then allocated to cover the expenses associated with extending the hours of medical clinics across the province. Would it be considered an effective reform?

The correct answer is: it depends. If there was clear evidence that patient health was being compromised because visits with physicians were too short, then longer visits might make sense. However, a mandatory lengthening of visits could just as easily lead to more time spent on small talk without improved patient care. It is more important to use existing time efficiently than to mandate longer visits.

Education reformers would be wise to take the same principle of efficiency and apply it to public education. All too often, proposed reforms are implemented whether warranted by the evidence or not. Lengthening the school day is one such reform. It pops up with regularity, particularly in the US.

As a case in point, five American states announced plans in 2012 to add at least 300 hours of instructional time to some of their schools each year. The three-year pilot program would involve more than 40 schools and approximately 20,000 students. The US education secretary at the time, Arne Duncan, a long-time advocate of longer school days, hailed this initiative as a "critical investment" that would prepare students for success in the 21st century.

The demand for longer school days finds support among some Canadian politicians as well. In the 2012 Quebec election, François Legault, leader of the Coalition Avenir Québec, proposed the addition of one extra hour to the school day for all secondary students. Under his proposal, high school students would be required to be in school from 9 a.m. to 5 p.m. every weekday. He suggested that the extra hour could be used for homework or extracurricular activities.

Interestingly, the main reason offered by Legault for a longer school day had little to do with improving student achievement. Rather, he focused on the need to synchronize the school day with the workdays of parents. He suggested that keeping students at school for longer could prevent them from getting into trouble when their parents were still at work.

However, before we jump on the longer-school-day bandwagon, it makes sense to ask whether the promise lives up to its hype. Do jurisdictions with more instructional time outperform jurisdictions where students spend less time in school?

They do not. For counter evidence we can look to Finland, a country where students consistently receive some of the highest reading scores in the world on the Programme for International Student Assessment (PISA). Finnish students spend less time in school than those in most other countries. School days are shorter, students attend on fewer days, and compulsory schooling only begins at the age of seven. The Finland example shows that academic success is possible without making students spend more time in school.

Lengthening the school day is a superficial solution to a more fundamental problem. While it is true that students who spend more time on-task usually experience greater success, there is no evidence that simply lengthening the school day results in more time on task. In other words, administrators should make better use of their existing time before trying to add more hours to the school day.

For example, students would be more successful at math if teachers taught basic math facts and standard algorithms, instead of the nebulous "new math" methods imposed by provincial curriculum guides. Similarly, reading levels would improve dramatically if students had more background knowledge about what they were reading. Unfortunately, most English language arts curriculum guides are virtually empty of content.

As Mike Schmoker points out in his book *Focus: Elevating the Essentials to Radically Improve Student Learning (2011)*, schools need a stronger focus on the essentials. If every school had a reasonably coherent curriculum, sound lessons, and purposeful reading and writing in every discipline, student achievement would improve. Unfortunately, schools are often distracted by initiatives that have little or nothing to do with their core mandate, thus taking time away from the essentials of learning.

If something isn't working, spending more time doing the same thing is unlikely to result in improvement. Schools should make better use of the time they currently have before adding hours to the school day.

COMMON SENSE NEEDED
ON SCHOOL SAFETY

IN 2012, THE horrific shooting at Sandy Hook Elementary School in Newtown, Connecticut, sparked a continent-wide discussion about school safety. This renewed interest in security was understandable – everyone wants students to be safe at school. Unfortunately, common sense seemed to be in short supply, as many proposed measures were not particularly helpful.

For example, the Ontario premier at the time, Dalton McGuinty, reacted to the Newtown massacre with a hasty pledge to implement a "locked-door policy" in all elementary schools. Along with requiring schools to lock their front doors when classes are in session, McGuinty's government wanted to spend CA\$10 million to make sure all schools were equipped with security cameras, buzzers, and locking doors.

Turning schools into miniature fortresses, however, does not guarantee student safety. The front doors at Sandy Hook Elementary were already locked – the killer simply shot through the front door and forced his way into the building. Short of turning every school into Fort Knox, it is nearly impossible to keep out a madman intent on inflicting damage.

Any public place, whether a movie theatre, shopping mall, church, or school is a possible target for someone determined to harm as many people as possible. No amount of planning can make any of these locations absolutely secure against intruders. The public needs to guard against politicians overreacting to tragedies that, fortunately, remain extremely rare, particularly in

Canada. The last thing we need is to turn our schools into virtual garrisons.

There are more immediate safety concerns. Rather than obsessing about the remote possibility of deranged gunmen entering schools, administrators should instead focus their attention on student discipline. Cracking down on bullying, maintaining orderly classrooms, and preventing physical altercations in hallways are the types of things on which all school administrators should focus. Students have the right to a safe and orderly learning environment.

Sadly, when it comes to student discipline, schools often veer into one of two extremes, neither of which is particularly helpful. At one end, some school districts implement draconian zero-tolerance policies that remove all discretion from students, teachers, and principals. While zero-tolerance policies may look good on paper, they often lead to absurd disciplinary actions. For example, a public school in Maryland suspended a six-year-old boy for pointing his finger at another student and saying "pow." It is unlikely that his fellow students feel much safer knowing their school is cracking down on dangerous finger guns!

Other zero-tolerance absurdities abound in the public school system. Students have been suspended for things ranging from bringing a butter knife to school to drawing a picture of a gun. In 2009, a six-year-old boy in Delaware was even ordered to attend reform school for 45 days for bringing a camping utensil to school. These incidents demonstrate how zero-tolerance removes the ability of teachers and principals to use their professional judgment, and leads to ridiculous decisions that make a mockery of the rules.

At the opposite extreme, some schools bend over backwards to accommodate troublemakers, even those who persistently disrupt the learning environment of others. Progressive educators often place so much emphasis on keeping troublemakers with their peers that they refuse to punish students who repeatedly disregard the most basic rules.

Alfie Kohn, a regular speaker at teacher professional development sessions, is a key proponent of this soft approach. In Kohn's view, schools should be fully egalitarian communities where rewards and punishments for students are nonexistent. According to Kohn, behaviour problems in schools disappear when teachers provide students with engaging lessons. However, his permissive idealism is based on a hopelessly naive understanding of human nature. Some students intentionally choose to disrupt class, bully their classmates, and destroy property, regardless of the quality of instruction they receive. Teachers who fail to enforce clear boundaries from the outset often end up with unruly classrooms.

In order to provide safer settings and more stable learning environments, schools must avoid the equally misguided extremes of zero-tolerance policies and permissive idealism. Rather, school administrators should set and enforce clear standards of behaviour for all students, and do so in a way that allows teachers to use their professional judgment. Rules need to be carefully designed, clearly explained, and consistently enforced.

Although no school can devise a foolproof plan to protect against every outside violent attack, all schools can and should establish a safe and orderly learning environment for their students. When it comes to school discipline, common sense is needed now more than ever.

PUT STUDENTS FIRST WHEN HIRING SUBSTITUTE TEACHERS

EVERY SPRING BRINGS the predictable spate of stories about the shortage of teaching jobs for new teachers in Canada. Declining student numbers mean the problem is particularly pronounced in Nova Scotia. As a result, many graduates languish for years on oversubscribed substitute lists.

Then, in the fall, comes a series of stories about how new teachers aren't getting enough substitute days. Invariably the blame is placed on retired teachers who continue to work as substitutes. According to the Nova Scotia Pension Agency, retired teachers can substitute for up to 69.5 days in a school year without any reduction to their pensions.

Because of their proven experience, retired teachers are often more popular with principals than untested new teachers. This doesn't sit well with a considerable number of new teachers. They argue that retired teachers have already had their chance to teach and are being selfish by taking positions that could be filled by new teachers. Some school administrators in neighbouring provinces agree with this concern.

For example, the Anglophone East school district in New Brunswick officially excludes retired teachers from its substitute list. During a CBC interview in December 2013, superintendent Gregg Ingersoll defended his district's policy. "They [retired teachers] have already done their career, whereas these new people, this is their only income," he explained.

On the other side of this issue, retired teachers claim that banning them from substitute lists amounts to age discrimination. This was the argument put forward by Fred Hall, a 67-year-old retired teacher who launched a human rights complaint in 2013 against the Anglophone East school district.

Thus, the issue is often presented as a choice between the interests of new teachers versus those of retired teachers. Lost in the shuffle is the one group whose interests should receive the most weight – students. Substitute teachers are called in to cover regular teachers for reasons ranging from professional development sessions to illness to personal leave days. This means students can expect to see substitute teachers many times throughout a year. When calling in a substitute, the first thing school administrators should consider is the impact on student learning.

For example, a retired math teacher with 30 years of successful teaching experience will often be the right person to step into a high school teacher's math class. On the other hand, a newly minted teacher who shows initiative and enthusiasm may be the right choice to take over a group of rambunctious Grade 8 students for the day. In all cases, the interests of students must be paramount.

As a result, substitute lists should be open to all qualified teachers, whether retired or not. Substitute teachers who know their subjects and can effectively manage classrooms should be called in as frequently as possible. Ineffective substitutes should be removed from the list entirely. The age of substitute teachers should be irrelevant; their ability to teach the students should be the only critcria.

Furthermore, school districts should avoid policies that unreasonably restrict the ability of administrators to hire the best substitute teachers. Forcing school principals to give an equal number of substitute opportunities to all teachers on an official list may benefit newly minted teachers, but it isn't in the best interests of students. When the regular teacher is absent, students deserve the substitute teacher who best provides a quality learning environment.

As for the plight of new teachers unable to find a job, there is no easy solution to this problem. Education faculties continue to graduate far more teachers than are needed in Nova Scotia schools. The ongoing decline in student numbers makes this problem even worse. Until things change, new graduates can expect to enter a difficult job market.

However, we cannot allow our sympathy for these new teachers to override the needs of students. Banning retired teachers from substitute lists may help some new teachers get a few extra days of work each year, but at the cost of depriving schools of many of the best available substitute teachers. This is not an acceptable trade-off.

When the news cycle brings the predictable stories about the plight of new teachers getting too little work, let's remember whose interests really matter. Principals should always put students first when hiring substitute teachers.

This article was originally published in 2014

WRONG MEDIUM FOR THIS STUDENT'S MESSAGE

"THE MEDIUM IS the message." That prescient observation was made in 1964 by the Canadian philosopher Marshall McLuhan. Basically, McLuhan meant that the way in which a message is transmitted is just as important as the message itself.

For example, those who watch a political leader's speech on television may react very differently from those who listen to the same speech on the radio. As a case in point, people who watched the famous Kennedy-Nixon presidential debates on television judged Kennedy the winner, while those who listened to the radio version preferred Nixon. Kennedy looked better on television and, for many viewers, this outweighed the substance of what he and Nixon had to say.

McLuhan died in 1980, long before the advent of the internet. Were he still alive today, he would probably be amazed at how the internet has confirmed his theory. Release one video on YouTube that goes viral and you can achieve instant worldwide fame.

In 2013, Jeff Bliss, an 18-year-old high school student in Texas, found out just how easy it is to become famous. Frustrated with the quality of instruction he was receiving in world history, he challenged his teacher in front of the class and let her know that he thought she was terrible at her job. One of his classmates recorded the exchange and uploaded it to YouTube. In only a few days, the 90-second video was watched more than 1.7 million times.

To be fair, much of what Bliss said during his rant makes sense. He talked about the need for teachers to be more active with their teaching and engage students face-to-face. He also correctly observed that simply handing out worksheets and expecting students to figure out everything themselves is not a good way to teach. Bliss apparently wanted to take a more active role in his own learning and this is commendable.

However, the way he went about expressing his views was not commendable. In fact, his poor attitude and disrespectful tone overshadowed the good points he made during his rant. "And if you would like, I'll teach you a little more so you can actually learn how to teach a freakin class," said Bliss as he left the room. These types of statements made him look arrogant and rude. No matter how upset Bliss was with the quality of instruction, insulting the teacher in front of the class was the wrong way to express his concerns.

During a radio interview, Bliss acknowledged that he did not discuss any of his concerns with the teacher before his public outburst. If Bliss really believed in the importance of face-to-face interaction, the least he could have done was meet with the teacher privately to express his concerns. Publicly attacking her without warning displayed poor judgment and undermined the point he wanted to make. In contrast, had Bliss expressed his concerns in private, registered a formal complaint with the school principal, or written a thoughtful article in his local newspaper, his message might have been taken more seriously.

In the internet age, it is more important than ever that we choose our medium carefully. For Bliss, this 90-second video was the wrong medium for his message.

SCHOOLS FOCUS TOO MUCH ON INDIVIDUALS

"EVERY STUDENT DESERVES a personalized learning experience that matches his or her unique learning style." This summarizes the obsession many schools have with individualized instruction. Heaven forbid that a teacher should prepare a lesson without considering the needs of each student.

As a result, instead of standing in front of the classroom and giving one explanation to all students, teachers often divide their classes into smaller groups and repeat the same lesson multiple times. In fact, teachers are often evaluated based on the degree to which they make use of "differentiated instruction" techniques. Unsurprisingly, this places enormous stress on teachers as they strive to meet the impossible goal of providing personalized instruction for each of the 25 or more students in their classrooms.

Not only is this obsession with individualized instruction stressful for teachers, but it also isn't particularly effective at improving student achievement.

In her comprehensive analysis of the research literature, published in the *International Guide to Student Achievement* (2013), the education researcher Catherine Scott noted that tailoring instruction to students' so-called learning styles is "a waste of precious teaching and learning time." Other experts, such as the cognitive psychologist Daniel Willingham, have come to the same conclusion.

Much of the problem stems from an excessive focus on educational psychology in teacher training and professional development. Teachers learn all about the psychological needs of individual students, but little about how to effectively manage a class of 25 or more students. What teachers really need is a little less psychology and a lot more sociology.

Teachers aren't hired as private tutors – their job is to teach groups of students. The best way for teachers to meet their needs is to engage the entire group with effective whole-class lessons. Of course, this is easier said than done, because it is not easy to manage the behaviour of 25 students while simultaneously providing engaging lessons. Unfortunately, despite the obvious importance of this skill, prospective teachers learn precious little in university about how to effectively teach large groups of students.

As Mike Schmoker points out in his book *Focus: Elevating the Essentials to Radically Improve Student Learning* (2011), a great deal of research has been conducted on what effective lessons look like. Teachers need to clearly explain new concepts, model how to solve problems, give students multiple opportunities to practice, and make sure students have mastered a new skill before moving on to the next level. In other words, they should make regular use of traditional, large-group, teacher-centred methods of teaching.

Jeanne Chall was a professor in the Harvard Graduate School of Education and director of the Harvard Reading Laboratory for more than 30 years. In her final book, *The Academic Achievement Challenge: What Really Works in the Classroom?* (2000), Chall examined the research evidence and compared the effectiveness of progressive student-centred education with traditional teacher-centred education. Her conclusion was clear: "Traditional, teacher-centred schools, according to research and practice, are more effective than progressive, student-centred schools for the academic achievement of most children." Not only that, but teacher-centred education was also especially beneficial for "children of less educated families, inner-city children, and those with learning difficulties at all social levels."

According to Chall, one of the advantages of teacher-centred classrooms is that they focus more "on preventing learning difficulties than on treating them with special procedures when found." Because teacher-centred instructors make regular use of whole-class instruction, they seek out methods and materials that are optimal for the entire group. When problems arise, these teachers can spend more time with the relatively few students experiencing difficulty while the other students work independently on their assignments.

In contrast, teachers in student-centred classrooms are expected at the outset to adapt their instruction to the individual learning styles of each student. As Chall points out, this is a highly inefficient way to teach because each student receives only a small amount of direct instruction each day. In addition, it is difficult to give additional time to academically weak students while also providing individualized instruction to all the other students.

Thus, schools should focus less on individualized instruction and more on teachers delivering effective whole-class lessons. This will help teachers to truly meet the needs of all students in their classrooms, especially those who are having difficulties with the lessons.

DISTRACTIONS ARE SOMETIMES GOOD FOR LEARNING

MOST TEACHERS AND students know the conventional dos and don'ts of proper studying habits. For example, you should find a quiet environment free of distractions. Don't play any background music and don't let your mind wander. And above all, don't stop working when you are making good progress.

These dos and don'ts exist because conventional wisdom has it that distractions are bad for learning. For a long time, this made intuitive sense and fit my notions about proper learning. But then I began to realize something – it didn't always match my own work habits or my experiences with students. In fact, I've found that I often do my best work when I start and stop frequently. For example, when writing a column like this one, I will often stop to check Facebook or surf the internet for a few minutes. Then I get up and walk around and mull things over in my mind.

These interruptions happen most frequently when I'm at a critical point in my work. And yet, somehow, I always manage to finish my columns on time and to an appropriate standard. Either I never learned how to work properly or something is wrong with the notion that distractions are always bad.

It turns out that my gradually shifting views about the merits of distraction now have significant scientific support. A book by the *New York Times* science reporter Benedict Carey does an excellent job of skewering many of the most common misconceptions about learning. *How We Learn* (2015) summarizes the research findings of cognitive psychology and applies them to everyday life.

For example, Carey describes an experiment that compared students who studied for a test in a quiet room with those who studied with jazz or Mozart playing in the background. Surprisingly, the students who studied in the quiet environment performed worse on the tests. Carey suggests that music and other background noises can actually enrich the study environment, as students form valuable associations that help them to remember the material.

Even interruptions may not be as bad as previously thought. Carey describes a major experimental study in which 164 students and teachers were given a series of short tasks to complete. However, instead of letting them proceed undisturbed, researchers interrupted the participants at random intervals. After the time was up, the participants were asked to list as many of the tasks as they could remember.

Researchers were surprised to discover that the participants remembered the interrupted tasks with almost twice the frequency of the uninterrupted tasks. Apparently, something about being interrupted caused them to remember that task more vividly. This was particularly true when the interruptions took place when the participants were most engrossed in the task at hand. In other words, one of the best ways to remember a task is to be interrupted right when you are in the middle of it.

According to Carey, interrupting our work at a critical moment and letting it percolate in our minds can help with the learning process. Carey explains that when we stop in the middle of a difficult problem and do something else for a while, we give our brains the opportunity to ponder it further and look for alternative solutions. So maybe it isn't the end of the world when a student responds to a text message or walks around the classroom for a moment before moving on to the next math problem.

There is, however, one important caveat. It is one thing for students to briefly distract themselves; it is another thing entirely when they are regularly distracted by the actions of others. Some distractions make it hard to concentrate and are very bad for learning. As a result, teachers must remain in control of their classrooms and provide students with a focused learning environment.

A balanced approach is needed. Students deserve a learning environment that is both structured and flexible. Some distractions are good for learning, while others are not. It's time to update the standard dos and don'ts of proper studying to reflect the findings of modern cognitive science.

CLASS SIZE IS NOT THE MOST IMPORTANT THING

IF YOU ASKED a group of teachers whether they would rather teach a class with 20 students or one with 30 students, most would pick the smaller class. All things being equal, it is easier to teach smaller classes than larger ones.

All things are never equal, however. There are many factors other than class size that impact student learning. And yet class size always seems to receive a disproportionate amount of attention, using up more oxygen.

In Ontario, for example, teacher unions have declared war on the Doug Ford government, largely because of the class size issue. In 2018, the previous education minister, Lisa Thompson, announced that the government would increase the average high school class from 22 to 28 students. But in 2019, the current education minister, Stephen Lecce, revised this target down to 25 students. Both announcements were met with fierce resistance from the teachers' unions.

It is not surprising that teacher unions advocate for smaller class sizes. Smaller classes mean that school boards need to hire more teachers, which means unions receive higher dues. Obviously, no union would publicly support a reduction in the number of dues-paying members.

On top of this, class size limits are very popular with rank-and-file teachers. That's because smaller classes mean less marking, more one-on-one time with students, and, especially, fewer report card comments to write. Although none of these things directly correlate with improved student achievement, they do contribute to the overall well-being of teachers, which is obviously an important consideration.

However, the issue is not whether smaller class sizes are popular with teachers and their unions. Instead, the question that needs to be answered is whether the benefits of reducing the average class size outweigh the costs that come with it. On this, the research is clear.

John Hattie, director of the Melbourne Education Research Institute at the University of Melbourne, is one of the top educational researchers in the world. He has analyzed thousands of research studies to determine the factors that have the largest impact on student achievement. Hattie has found that capping class size brings a huge cost, but, contrary to what the unions often claim, it has only a small benefit.

In the *International Guide to Student Achievement* (2013), Hattie concludes that "there is a voluminous literature that does not support the claim that learning outcomes are markedly enhanced when class sizes are reduced." He explains that the research studies varied widely in design and methodology, but all agreed on one thing – the effects of reducing class size are "quite small."

In one such study, Drs. Wei Li and Spyros Konstantopoulos used data from 14 European countries to evaluate the impact of various class sizes on fourth-grade students' achievement in mathematics. Their findings were published in 2017 in the peer-reviewed journal *School Effectiveness and School Improvement.* Specifically, Li and Konstantopoulos found that "class-size effects are generally non-significant."

One thing that is clear is that reducing class sizes is the costliest education reform provincial governments can undertake. Ontario currently has approximately 115,000 full-time teachers. Decreasing the average class size by only 10% would cost Ontario taxpayers an additional CA$11.5 billion a year. This number does not include the cost of constructing additional classrooms or the inevitable administration costs that come with having more teachers.

It makes little sense to spend a huge amount of money on something that has, at best, a modest impact on student achievement. Money that goes to hiring additional teachers cannot go to buying new textbooks, upgrading school facilities, providing professional development to teachers, putting more educational assistants in classrooms, or improving student access to technology. Governments would be wise to invest more resources in lower-cost initiatives that potentially have a much larger impact on student achievement.

For example, the Ontario government has announced its intention to replace discovery math with a back-to-basics math curriculum. This should not be hard to do. Replacing the useless *Math Makes Sense* textbook series with JUMP Math, a program that properly emphasizes the mastery of math facts and the use of standard algorithms, would go a long way toward improving the math performance of students. The reality is that a class of 30 students using JUMP Math will almost certainly outperform a class of 15 students who continue to use discovery math textbooks.

Revising the curriculum in other subject areas to have a stronger emphasis on content knowledge would also benefit students. Building up the knowledge capacity of students in all subject areas is important for developing reading comprehension, essential for improving critical thinking skills, and a great way to reduce the academic gap between students from rich neighbourhoods and those from poor ones.

The class-size discussion has consumed too much oxygen in the education debate. It's time for other, more important issues to finally be addressed.

IMPROVE TEACHER WORKING CONDITIONS BY DUMPING BAD IDEAS

TEACHERS IN NEWFOUNDLAND and Labrador are stressed. In a presentation to the Premier's Task Force on Improving Educational Outcomes, the Newfoundland and Labrador Teachers' Association presented compelling data, both scientific and anecdotal, showing that working conditions for classroom teachers are not good.

Teachers in the province have classes of many students with severe behavioural problems, significant cognitive disabilities, and diverse academic skills. With only limited support, teachers find it difficult to provide adequate instruction. They are pressured to develop multiple lesson plans for each class to accommodate the variety of individual needs.

Frankly, this expectation is unrealistic – it sets teachers up for failure.

Over the past 30 years, Newfoundland and Labrador, like other provinces, has moved to an inclusive education model. In principle, this makes sense. Students deserve to be educated with their peers. While some students require specialized support, there are good reasons to include all students in regular classrooms to the greatest degree possible.

However, problems arise when faulty educational theories are pushed on teachers who have little choice but to comply. The worst, without a doubt, is that teachers should replace structured, whole-class teaching with project-based discovery learning. Even though there is a wealth of evidence supporting traditional teaching techniques, school administrators, government officials, and education professors often push an ideological agenda against traditional methods.

Interestingly, traditional classrooms are exactly what many students with learning disabilities benefit from the most. A structured classroom with desks facing the front and a clear and focused lesson delivered by a competent teacher provide an excellent environment in which to learn. Instead, teachers are told to seat their students in groups, facing each other, and let them learn together at their own pace. This is a recipe for disaster, particularly in classrooms with students who have behavioural challenges.

Differentiated instruction is a fad often pushed on teachers. Based largely on the work of Carol

Ann Tomlinson, an American educator, differentiated instruction tells teachers to adapt their lessons to the individual learning styles of each student. Although this sounds good in theory, it falls apart in practice, since it is impossible for teachers to design multiple effective lessons for each of the courses they teach every single day.

What ends up happening is that teachers divide their classes into groups and try to give mini-lessons to each of these small groups, while hoping that the remaining students remain focused enough on their independent assignments to not cause too much distraction. It is a horrendously inefficient way to teach and it creates an impossible workload for teachers. Teachers burn out in short order. To make matters worse, there is no empirical evidence that differentiated instruction actually works.

For example, Bryan Goodwin of Mid-Continent Research for Education and Learning stated in a 2010 report, *Changing the Odds for Student Success: What Matters Most*, that there is a "dearth of evidence supporting differentiated instruction" and that "[the] extent to which teachers differentiate instruction in their classrooms is not a key variable in student success." Unfortunately, teachers rarely hear about this evidence.

One of the key faults of differentiated instruction is that it is based on the even faultier notion of individual learning styles. While many teachers accept the gospel that some students are visual learners, some are auditory learners, and others are tactile-kinesthetic learners, there is not a shred of evidence supporting this theory. John Hattie, director of the Melbourne Education Research

Institute at the University of Melbourne, has reviewed thousands of studies about student achievement. In his book *Visible Learning for Teachers* (2012), Hattie bluntly states that there is "zero supporting evidence" for learning styles.

The damage caused by this failed theory is substantial. Instead of providing well-designed whole-class lessons, teachers waste hours trying to adapt to the so-called learning styles of each student. As a result, they end up working harder, getting worse results, and burning themselves out.

Things need to change. Instead of being forced to adopt failed theories and foolish fads, teachers should be empowered to use the most effective methods. Dumping bad ideas and bad practices would go a long way toward improving the effectiveness of teachers in Newfoundland and Labrador and beyond.

This article was originally published in 2017

GIVING TEACHERS A VOICE IN PROFESSIONAL DEVELOPMENT

TEACHING IS A challenging job. Anyone who has spent a few days in a school knows that teachers have a lot of demands placed upon them. Their responsibilities often go far beyond classroom instruction, from dealing with disruptive student behaviour to organizing extracurricular activities to supervising hallways and playgrounds.

In order to face these and other challenges, teachers must continually improve their skills through professional development. This is far from easy, particularly since teachers must sort through the myriad of competing claims in the education world. Education fads are a dime a dozen and they are becoming more prevalent.

Much of the problem stems from the substandard training provided by university education faculties, where pre-service teachers are exposed to a plethora of fads, most of which are really bad ideas. Individual learning styles, multiple intelligences, no-zero policies, and 21st-century skills are but a few examples. Sadly, these and other fads are often reinforced at their professional development sessions after they become full-fledged teachers.

Fortunately, some teachers are pushing back against these bad ideas. One such group of teachers met in Toronto in 2017 at the researchED conference. These professional development conferences – started in 2013 in Britain by Tom Bennett, a well-known teacher and education writer – are held by teachers for teachers. None of the organizers or speakers at researchED receives any compensation for their work. They participate because they believe in what they are doing – helping other teachers to improve their teaching.

Teachers from across Canada came to Toronto to hear from a variety of experts. Among the presenters were Dr. Daniel Ansari, Canada research chair in developmental cognitive neuroscience at Western University; Dr. John Mighton, mathematician and founder of JUMP Math; Martin Robinson, author of *Trivium 21c: Preparing Young People for the Future With Lessons From the Past*;

and Dr. Stan Kutcher, psychiatry professor at Dalhousie University and expert in adolescent mental health. In addition, a variety of classroom teachers led workshops about how they integrate the best research into their classrooms.

What makes researchED different from typical professional development conferences is that teachers are given a real voice in the discussions. They are not simply expected to give lip service to the latest fad, but are actually encouraged to openly challenge any claims made by the presenters. For many teachers, researchED is their first real opportunity to engage with the research in an environment that encourages critical thinking and honest debate.

I led a session at the Toronto researchED conference, so I had the opportunity to intellectually engage with teachers from all over Canada. Sadly, many of them are under such pressure by school administrators to conform to the latest fads that they cannot make their identities publicly known. In a desperate attempt to get their voices heard, they often resort to anonymous Twitter handles or anonymous blog posts. Thankfully, researchED gave them a chance to meet like-minded teachers and researchers from across Canada. Now they know they are not alone.

During one of the sessions, Sachin Maharaj, a teacher with the Toronto District School Board, delivered an excellent presentation about teacher professionalism and career development. He made it clear that in order for teachers to become full-fledged professionals, they must take an active role in their own professional development. He also argued that it should be possible for teachers to enhance their pay and their status without moving out of teaching and into consulting or administration. After all, the best teachers belong in classrooms, not in offices.

Imagine what improvements we might see in Canadian education if all teacher professional development sessions were like researchED. Instead of listening to canned presentations and hearing about useless fads, teachers would actively review the latest research evidence and debate the pros and cons of using these strategies with their colleagues. Considering how much emphasis is placed on critical thinking in schools today, it is ironic that so many teacher professional development sessions minimize debate and emphasize conformity.

Hopefully, conferences like researchED become the norm rather than the exception in teacher professional development. No teacher should have to create an anonymous Twitter account in order to be heard.

STUDENTS SHOULD NOT BE ENCOURAGED TO SKIP SCHOOL

WHETHER 'TIS NOBLER for students to suffer the tests and assignments of regular class, or to take up arms in the name of social justice and by skipping, thus to oppose injustice?

OK, the question of whether students should skip class in the name of social justice may not be quite as existential as the one facing Shakespeare's Hamlet, but it's still important. For many young people, Greta

Thunberg, the Swedish teenager who organized the school climate strike, is a hero worthy of emulation. A growing number of students around the world are following Thunberg's example by walking out of class to raise concerns about climate change.

In 2019, thousands of students across Canada walked out of class to participate in rallies calling on politicians to take tougher action on climate change. Considering the strong correlation between regular school attendance and academic achievement, one might assume that educators would discourage students from skipping class. Unfortunately, not only do some educators have little problem with these protests, but some of them actively encourage their students to forsake their educational responsibilities.

For example, at its 2019 Spring Representative Assembly, the British Columbia Teachers' Federation passed the following resolution: "That the BCTF support the student Climate Strike on the next worldwide day of action that is organized to demand action on the climate emergency." In an email sent in September 2019, the BCTF encouraged teachers to help students organize an event in their local communities and to "avoid scheduling tests or assignment due dates on the day of the climate strike."

Even some school boards are lending tacit approval to this event. On its website, the Toronto District School Board states that while the student climate strike isn't a TDSB-sanctioned event, teachers have been instructed to avoid scheduling tests or other assessments for that day. In other words, the TDSB wants to ensure that students who skip class that day don't suffer any academic penalty.

However, there are a number of reasons why teachers' unions and school boards should rethink their support for these student strikes. First, class time really does matter. There are a limited number of days in the school year and teachers need to make the best use of the time they have. Encouraging students to skip class sends the unfortunate message that attendance doesn't really matter.

The fact is that no matter how passionate students might be about a social cause, it's unlikely that most students know much about it – they are surely not experts. That's because expertise needs to be developed through hard work and it usually takes a long time to master a skill. Skipping class to engage in protests, regardless of how worthy the issue seems to be, short-circuits the learning process. Holding up a sign at a protest might be more exciting than learning about the different cloud types in a geography class, but this doesn't change the fact that knowledge acquisition remains an essential part of learning. Schools need to focus on educating students, not on facilitating protests.

Teachers should also keep in mind that student strikes impact all students, not just the ones who skip classes. That's because teachers know it is pointless to introduce new material when a significant number of students are absent. Simply put, the material would need to be retaught anyway. Thus, the students who choose not to protest end up just as shortchanged as the students who skip class. It gets even worse when teachers cancel classes to support protests. In that situation, neither the responsible nor the irresponsible students can attend class.

In addition, if students are allowed to skip class to attend climate strikes, they should be allowed to skip classes for other protests. However, we know that teachers' unions and school boards wouldn't be nearly as supportive if students wanted to skip classes to attend an anti-abortion demonstration or a pro-oil-pipeline rally. It hardly encourages critical thinking when teachers encourage students to skip school only for the protests they happen to personally support.

There is a better way. Instead of skipping school, students should organize protests on the weekend when school isn't in session. This would be a great way for them to show that they aren't at the protest rallies just to miss class, but are genuinely concerned about the issue. When large numbers of students give up income from their part-time jobs or sacrifice time with their friends in order to attend a protest rally, then we know they are serious.

COMMON SENSE

~ 8 ~

THE POLITICS OF EDUCATION

THE 1995 FILM *Mr. Holland's Opus* tells the inspirational story of a fictional music teacher, Glenn Holland. His ultimate goal is to become a composer, but by the age of 30 he has not made a breakthrough and reluctantly accepts a teaching position in order to provide for his family. Holland experiences many challenges in his teaching career, but eventually comes to embrace his role as an educator. The movie shows that throughout his 30 years in music, Holland impacts the lives of thousands of students and inspires many of them to pursue careers in music.

However, near the end of the movie Holland receives some devastating news from the school principal. The board of education has mandated that all schools in the district must reduce their budgets by 10%. In response, the principal cuts the music and drama programs, which forces Holland to take early retirement. He attempts to fight the decision by making a presentation to the school board, but his pleas fall on deaf ears.

Mr. Holland's Opus may be fictional, but it accurately shows that it is impossible to separate politics from education. Although it sounds noble when teachers say they care only about teaching and will let others deal with politics, the reality is that politics impacts all teachers, whether they realize it or not.

In Canada, provincial governments have control over education and that is the level where the big decisions are made. In the US, states have the same control. Most of the articles in this chapter describe a series of education changes taking place in the province of Alberta, but they apply to many other provinces and states. The first article considers the *Inspiring Education* report that proposed a transformative shift in education. Unfortunately, the report was transformative in the wrong ways, as it basically rehashed the progressive approach of the 18th-century philosopher Jean-Jacques Rousseau. Subsequent articles trace how this one report continues to negatively affect Alberta's schools.

Other articles address political issues in the provinces of Manitoba and Ontario. Both these provinces faced significant financial challenges and the decisions the governments made had a real impact on classroom teachers. These articles show that it is important for teachers to pay attention to politics and to be prepared to speak up at appropriate times. If their voices are not heard early in the process, it might be too late at the end.

The exact challenges vary depending on what country, province, or state you are in, but the broader issues remain generally consistent. Governments set the overall education direction for schools, and teachers should not be afraid to make their voices heard.

'INSPIRING' REPORT IS RECYCLED EDU-BABBLE

ALBERTA'S PUBLIC EDUCATION system needs to undergo an informed transformation over the next 20 years. At least, that is the dramatic conclusion of the *Inspiring Education* report, released in 2010.

What really stands out about this report is that it is long on edu-babble and short on substance. *Inspiring Education* states that students need to "learn how to learn," become "life-long learners," and "apply multiple literacies." To achieve these goals, schools should move away from the "industrial model" of school, become more "learner-centred," and have a greater emphasis on "experiential learning."

Despite the fact that Alberta students regularly outperform those from other provinces on academic achievement tests, the report concludes that students are not well-served by the current education system. "Very few Albertans believe today's children are learning in a manner that responds to current or emerging realities," state the authors of the report.

Inspiring Education explains that in today's information-based society, knowledge increases at an exponential rate. As a result, schools need to place less emphasis on covering content and more emphasis on teaching students how to look up information on the internet. It does not come as a surprise that the report also recommends moving away from traditional grade and subject divisions and towards a more integrated curriculum model.

Alberta's education minister may believe that this report outlines a new approach to public education, but the reality is that it is yet another manifestation of an anti-knowledge romantic progressivism that goes all the way back to the 18th-century philosopher Jean-Jacques Rousseau. This is the same thinking that brought us failed innovations such as open-area classrooms, the whole-language approach to reading instruction, and the "new" math.

Contrary to what the authors of *Inspiring Education* appear to believe, the increase in the amount of knowledge available does not make the learning of specific facts unnecessary. The claim that schools should teach students how to look up information rather than pass on specific facts to them is fundamentally misguided. It is by acquiring extensive background knowledge of their culture – what the education author E. D. Hirsch, Jr. refers to as core knowledge – that students make sense of the world around them.

Nevertheless, the report asserts that schools less focused on content make it possible for students to think more deeply about important issues. What advocates of this approach forget is that it is impossible to think deeply about something you know nothing about. Critical thinking is most likely to be done by those students who possess the most extensive knowledge of the subject in question. This fact makes it all the more essential that we immerse students in content-rich instruction.

Another area of concern is the way in which the report virtually ignores the importance of standardized testing. Alberta has the most advanced standardized testing regime in Canada, and there is good reason to believe that this is largely responsible for the fact that Alberta students do so well on international comparisons of academic achievement. Considering that Alberta leads the way in this field, it is disconcerting that this report nowhere acknowledges the importance of maintaining these exams.

The report also suffers from a lack of inspiration in another key area: school choice. Although it pays lip service to the importance of flexibility and local control of schools, it does not mention making it easier for parents to choose the school that their children attend. This is a curious omission considering that Alberta is home to more than a dozen thriving charter schools and its second-largest school division, Edmonton Public Schools, has for more than three decades successfully made the expansion of school choice central to its educational philosophy.

Transformative change in education does not come about by dressing up the failed romantic progressive ideologies of the past in a fancy CA$3 million document filled with edu-babble. *Inspiring Education* is neither inspiring nor focused on real education.

SECRECY ON SCHOOLS IS INSULTING

FOR MANY YEARS, Manitoba has had a reputation as a middle-of-the-road province with an adversity to extremes. In one area of provincial policy, however, Manitoba boldly stands alone. It is the only province that stubbornly refuses to make information about student academic performance available to the general public.

The Atlantic Institute for Market Studies and the Frontier Centre for Public Policy recently released a report on public schools in Manitoba and Saskatchewan. In order to compile this report, these think tanks needed information such as school graduation rates, attendance records, and student performance on standards tests.

Whereas Saskatchewan willingly released most of the requested information, Manitoba Education and Literacy refused to cooperate. As a result, the report contains virtually no useful information about Manitoba high schools. Information that is routinely available in other parts of Canada remains locked away in this province.

The education minister, Nancy Allan, made a number of media appearances in an attempt to justify her government's stance against accountability. During a CBC Radio interview, Allan offered up her usual talking points. In her initial argument, Allan pointed out that the province had published a report called *A Profile of Student Learning and Performance in Manitoba* on its website. This report is limited to providing student data on a province-wide basis, making it useful only to people naive enough to believe that all schools in Manitoba are exactly the same.

When challenged on this point, Allan argued there was no benefit to breaking down the information any further. According to the education minister, if that kind of data were available to the public then it might be misused by think tanks wishing to rank schools on the basis of performance.

With all due respect to Allan, that is an absurd reason to keep information away from the public. Using this logic, Manitoba should also prevent regional health authorities from releasing any regional health care data just in case some think tank decides to "misuse" the information and ranks hospitals on the basis of performance. This paternalistic approach to information is insulting to the public. We don't need Allan or anyone else from the government telling us that these data are being kept from us for our own good.

In addition, there is good reason for concern about student academic achievement in Manitoba. The 2009 Programme for International Student Assessment (PISA) ranked Manitoba second-last among Canadian provinces in reading and mathematics. In fact, this assessment showed that province-wide academic results had steadily declined since the New Democratic Party took power in 1999. The government probably thinks it has good reason to keep academic data away from Manitobans, particularly during an election year.

It was ironic that, during the same radio interview, Allan pointed to the strong PISA results from Finland as proof that standards tests weren't necessary in Manitoba. Finland, she noted, does not have a lot of standards tests and yet still performs very well on international comparisons of student achievement.

Aside from the obvious irony of using results from a standardized test to prove we don't need standardized testing, there are other reasons to be cautious about comparisons with Finland. The population in Finland is considerably more homogeneous than in Canada and schooling is only compulsory until the end of Grade 9. Local schools also have considerably more autonomy than they do in Manitoba.

Manitoba needs to follow the example of other provinces and make academic achievement data available to the public. People have a right to know how their schools are doing.

This article was originally published in 2011

ONTARIO SHOULD IMPLEMENT DRUMMOND RECOMMENDATIONS

IF THE STATUS quo prevails, Ontario's public education system is fiscally unsustainable. That is the dire conclusion of the recently released Drummond report.

The numbers in the report are staggering. Over the previous decade, student enrolment declined by approximately 120,000, while teaching and non-teaching staff grew by 24,000. From 2002–03 to 2011–12, per-pupil funding increased annually by 4.6%, well above the rate of inflation.

This paints a picture of a system in urgent need of reform. Costly initiatives such as reduced class sizes and full-day kindergarten may be popular with teachers' unions and parents, but they have little direct impact on student achievement. It should come as little surprise that the Drummond report comes down hard on these types of initiatives.

With 90% of primary (kindergarten to Grade 3) classes numbering 20 students or less and the remainder capped at 23 students, expenditures on teaching and non-teaching staff salaries have increased substantially. Smaller class sizes mean schools need more teachers, more educational assistants, and more classroom space. Such a costly initiative could only be justified if there was strong evidence of its effectiveness.

However, the educational research is clear. Reducing class sizes has, at best, only a modest impact on student achievement. John Hattie is an education professor who has reviewed literally hundreds of research studies about student achievement. In his book *Visible Learning* (2009), Hattie concludes that the results of reducing class sizes are "systematically small."

Advocates of smaller class sizes invariably respond by pointing to the Tennessee Student-Teacher Achievement Ratio (STAR) longitudinal study from the 1990s. The study purported to show that students in smaller classes made greater gains in literacy and mathematics than students in larger classes. However, many experts who reviewed this study found significant flaws with its design. For example, schools were not selected randomly and students often moved from one control group to another.

In addition, the small classes in the STAR report had only 13–17 students, while the large classes had 22–25 students. Thus, even if we accept that the STAR report shows the benefits of smaller class sizes, this definition only applies to classes of 17 students or less. Since the Ontario government has no intention of reducing class sizes to that level, the relevance of the STAR study to Ontario's situation is questionable.

The Drummond report also recommends that Ontario's government cancel its planned full-day kindergarten program. It's not hard to see why. Once implemented across the province, this program will cost more than CA$1.5 billion per year. Although advocates believe full-day kindergarten benefits students, there is little evidence at this point of its long-term effectiveness.

As a case in point, the failure of the massive Head Start program in the US should serve as a caution to those who tout the benefits of full-day kindergarten. Head Start began in 1965 as a preschool program aimed at disadvantaged three- and four-year-olds. A thorough evaluation of this program was conducted in 2010, concluding that any modest benefits from the initiative vanished by the end of Grade 1. In other words, the students who participated in Head Start ended up no better off than those who did not.

Another recommendation in the Drummond report is to reduce the number of non-teaching positions by 70%. In the past decade, the number of educational assistants, consultants, office staff, and curriculum coordinators has grown substantially, although the number of students has decreased. School boards and provincial education departments should not be allowed to grow their fiefdoms at taxpayer expense.

Finally, the Drummond report makes an important observation about teacher compensation. It notes that teachers receive automatic salary increases when they complete additional years of university education, even if these courses have nothing to do with their work in the classroom. A better approach would be to grant these increases only when an independent body determines that the additional qualifications will benefit students. Although a modest change, it would open the door to future adjustments to the teacher salary grid.

Let's hope the Ontario government takes the Drummond report seriously. Improving student achievement and bringing the budget into balance are two very good reasons to accept the report's recommendations.

This article was originally published in 2012

A TIME FOR CHOOSING IN ALBERTA EDUCATION

THE PUBLIC EDUCATION system in Alberta has long been the envy of Canada. Students in this province regularly outperform students from other provinces on national and international standardized achievement tests. Alberta students have some of the best results in the world.

Their impressive achievement does not happen by chance. Alberta has consciously chosen to implement education policies that focus on results. A case in point is the standardized tests that students write in grades 3, 6, 9, and 12. The Grade 3 tests evaluate literacy and numeracy skills, the grades 6 and 9 tests focus on the four core subjects (math, science, language arts, and social studies), while the Grade 12 diploma exams evaluate the skills of students in a variety of subjects.

Alberta has the most comprehensive standardized testing program in Canada and these tests play a key role in measuring student achievement and identifying areas where improvement is needed. Without standardized testing, it is almost impossible for policymakers to accurately evaluate the achievement of students across the province and to identify areas that may need improvement.

Another area in which Alberta leads the way is school choice. In 1994, the provincial government allowed the creation of charter schools and today there are 13 of these schools in existence, representing approximately 1% of Alberta students. Charter schools are publicly funded but operate autonomously from school boards. Some charter schools, most notably Foundations for the Future Charter Academy in Calgary, are highly successful and have long waiting lists of prospective students.

The Edmonton Public School Board has made choice the foundation of its approach to education. Its open boundary system makes it possible for students to attend schools outside of their traditional neighbourhood catchment areas. Within the public school system, students have the option of attending schools that specialize in areas such as the arts, sports, and Aboriginal culture. Even faith-based schools exist within the public system. Making wider choices available to families strengthens the public education system.

During the current 2012 election campaign, voters in Alberta are faced with a stark choice when it comes to education policy. Under the leadership of Premier Alison

Redford, the Progressive Conservatives are poised to undo much of what has made Alberta's education system so successful. As a case in point, shortly before winning the Progressive Conservative (PC) leadership, Redford promised to abolish standardized testing in grades 3 and 6. Although she has not yet acted on this pledge, it is almost certain to happen if her government wins re-election.

Redford's campaign promises also reveal a top-down approach to public education that undermines local input. Since the Alberta Teachers' Association played a key role in helping her to win the PC leadership race last year, it will continue to have disproportionate influence over her administration. Her recent pledge to spend CA$2.4 billion constructing 50 new schools and renovating an additional 70 schools further removes decision-making from the local level. And while the PC election platform contains platitudes about empowering parents, there are no concrete pledges to expand school choice in Alberta or even to preserve the choices currently available. This lack of commitment to an important part of Alberta's education system is reason for concern.

In contrast, the Wildrose Party has a much stronger emphasis on local autonomy and school choice. Its platform explicitly promises to uphold educational choice in Alberta and to give greater decision-making powers to local schools. Its pledge to depoliticize the construction of new schools with a public and objective funding formula stands in stark contrast to the top-down and seemingly arbitrary approach of the current government.

As for standardized testing, Wildrose promises to replace the provincial achievement tests with a new standardized assessment model. Although this pledge needs to be fleshed out, the party's firm commitment to releasing achievement data to the public means any new model cannot be radically different from existing standardized tests. Most notably, Wildrose has not made any foolish pledges to scrap standardized testing at some grade levels.

Alberta voters should make education a top priority when they go to the polls. The choice is stark. The continued success of Alberta's school system and the future of Alberta's children may depend on the outcome.

This article was originally published in 2012

ALBERTA SCHOOLS ARE GETTING WORSE, NOT BETTER

THERE IS AN old saying that insanity is doing the same thing over and over again and expecting different results. By this standard, Alberta's provincial government must be insane – at least when it comes to public education reform.

Over the past decade, Alberta Education has initiated a radical overhaul of public education. Less reliance on standardized testing, a discovery-based math curriculum, reduced emphasis on academic content, and new grading schemes are but a few examples. But the results have not been encouraging.

In fact, recently released data from the 2012 Programme for International Student Assessment

(PISA) paints a grim picture of a province in academic decline. Nowhere has this decline been more precipitous than in math. Whereas Alberta students used to lead Canada in math scores, now they are merely average. Without a dramatic shift back to the academic basics, this downward trend will almost certainly continue.

The education minister, Jeff Johnson, has paid lip service to the problem but given no indication that he plans to reverse course. Of course, there was little reason to expect otherwise. As one of the key architects behind the 2010 *Inspiring Education* report, Johnson has a vested interest in continuing his department's current direction.

However, once you strip away the report's soaring rhetoric and cut through the edu-babble, *Inspiring Education* is merely a recycled presentation of the failed progressive ideologies of the past. Its pledge to move education away from learning specific knowledge and skills to a process of inquiry and discovery has been the typical rallying cry of progressive educators for more than a century.

For example, back in 1918, the educational theorist William Heard Kilpatrick outlined his "project method" in an article published in the *Teachers College Record*. Just like *Inspiring Education*, Kilpatrick advocated the integration of subject areas and downplayed the importance of academic content. In fact, *Inspiring Education* is so similar to Kilpatrick's philosophy that it could have been written by him, were he still alive. Sadly, Kilpatrick's progressive philosophy had a profoundly negative impact on public education in North America. Although a small number of education professors opposed his philosophy, most education schools adopted his ideas and passed them on to future generations of teachers.

Until recently, Alberta stood out as a beacon of common sense against the onslaught of this progressive ideology. Its commitment to parental choice, rigorous standardized testing, and solid academic content made Alberta unique in Canada. Alberta students had the highest PISA scores in Canada and some of the best in the world. Unfortunately, as the Alberta government continues to dismantle the best features of the province's once proud school system, students are paying the price.

Teachers frustrated with the decline in academic standards shouldn't expect any help from the Alberta Teachers' Association (ATA). In its 2012 research update, *A Great School for All: Transforming Education in Alberta*, the ATA praised the *Inspiring Education* report as "a positive first step." Incredibly, the ATA wants to go even further down the progressive path of education reform.

Much of the ATA's report is an endorsement of Finland's education system and the so-called "fourth way" paradigm of the American educator Andy Hargreaves. This admiration of Finland stems from the way in which the country's schools incorporate aspects of progressive ideology into their practice. As a result, the ATA seeks to remake Alberta's education system in the image of Finland.

Unfortunately for them, Finland has dropped from its once high standing in PISA. While still one of the higher performing nations, Finland's results have declined over the past decade and the country now scores at almost exactly the same level as Canada. Asian countries such as Singapore and South Korea, both of which use traditional methods of instruction, have significantly surpassed Finland.

To make matters worse, as the Alberta government continues to water down academic standards, some school boards are replacing percentage grades on report cards with confusing and imprecise letter grades. This makes it difficult for parents to understand how their children are doing. Acting on the advice of misguided assessment gurus, some schools have even adopted rigid no-zero policies.

If the Alberta government continues on the failed progressive path of reform, academic achievement will continue to decline. Without a major course correction, things are going to get a lot worse before they get better. Insanity, as they say, is doing the same thing over and over again and expecting different results. Alberta's parents deserve better.

This article was originally published in 2013

EVERYTHING IS CHANGING, EXCEPT FAILED EDUCATION FADS

"EVERYTHING IS CHANGING." So states the two-minute promotional video on the Alberta government's Inspiring Education website. It describes the need to "prepare Alberta's students for this unknown and unknowable future" and notes that "we cannot predict what work will look like in ten years, let alone what skills will be required."

In other words, the Alberta government now wants to prepare students for an "unknowable" future. Because traditional learning no longer meets this goal, the narrator cheerfully concludes, "We're changing everything."

Confused? You should be. The government plans to scrap the top-performing education system in Canada and replace it with a system that helps students develop unknown skills for jobs that don't yet exist in some unknowable future. Only in education is such claptrap accepted as sensible policy.

Imagine if another government department featured such a ridiculous video on its website. Would anyone take Inspiring Health seriously if a video proclaimed "we're changing everything" because "we cannot predict what medicine will look like in ten years"? Or how about an Inspiring Justice video stating that the justice system must "prepare Alberta's criminals for an unknown and unknowable future"? For some reason, education is the one profession where it is acceptable to regularly throw out proven practices and replace them with new and unproven theories that have no evidence to support them.

Remember open-area classrooms? In the 1970s, Alberta constructed elementary schools without walls. Classes met in open areas separated by dividers. The theory was that open classes would allow exciting new "team teaching" opportunities and create a buzz of learning throughout the school. In reality, many students couldn't handle the noise and disruption, so governments eventually built classroom walls at great expense. Despite the obvious problems with open-area classrooms, this theory dominated North America for years and did great damage to the learning of millions of students. For a profession that allegedly values critical thinking, it is remarkable that such a misguided theory was adopted so uncritically.

Failed education fads are not a thing of the past. Right now, Alberta students and their parents are suffering from the discovery math approach. Instead of making students memorize multiplication tables and learn the most efficient algorithms for solving math problems, discovery math encourages students to invent their own strategies and techniques. As a result, parents spend hours at home helping their kids to figure out convoluted word problems that don't make sense. Not surprisingly, the math scores of Alberta students have steadily declined since the formal introduction of discovery math in 2008.

What do Inspiring Education, open-area classrooms, and discovery math have in common? They are manifestations of the same failed educational philosophy – progressivism.

Progressives have a naively optimistic belief in the ability of students to direct their own learning. They dislike teacher-led classrooms and want each teacher to be a guide on the side, rather than a sage on the stage. They prefer to focus on the process of learning and de-emphasize specific curriculum content. Any rote learning is derided as "drill and kill."

Inspiring Education proposes another version of this failed philosophy. Parents who are frustrated with discovery math can look forward to other subject areas becoming equally confusing. For example, science courses will focus less on learning key scientific facts and theories, and more on students discovering things for themselves. History courses will focus more on social justice activism than on providing students with an accurate understanding of the past.

Equally concerning is the Inspiring Education video's nonsensical claim that we have no idea what skills will be required in the future. In reality, virtually everyone agrees that students will still need to know how to read and write, do math, and have a basic understanding of Canadian history and governance. These disciplines and skills will be just as useful 20 years from now as they are today and were 100 years ago.

If the Alberta government is determined to stick with its mantra that "everything is changing," it should change its Inspiring Education campaign into something useful. Building on Alberta's proven strengths would be a much better strategy than tearing everything down just for the sake of change.

DESPITE PROMISES, FUZZY EDUCATION AGENDA ENDURES

DURING THE 2014 Progressive Conservative leadership race, Jim Prentice said Alberta schools needed to focus on the academic basics. Then, when he became premier of Alberta, he appointed Gordon Dirks as minister of education, someone known to be sympathetic to traditional education ideas.

In this appointment, Prentice signalled a willingness to change course from the previous government's disastrous Inspiring Education initiative. Parents looking for change had further cause for hope when Prentice shuffled Greg Bass out of the job of deputy minister of education. With Bass's removal, Alberta Education lost its most prominent discovery-learning evangelist.

However, despite a new premier, a new minister of education and a new deputy minister, the Inspiring Education initiative remains intact. Its nonsensical *Everything is Changing* video can still be viewed on the department's website and the supporting documents also remain. If Prentice genuinely wants to change direction in Alberta Education, he must remove this material from his government's website.

Even more concerning is the lack of action on the provincial math curriculum. Although the previous education minister, Jeff Johnson, reluctantly agreed to revise the math curriculum by requiring students to memorize basic math facts, he did not go nearly far enough. Fuzzy math textbooks, such as *Math Makes Sense*, remain in use and there is still no requirement for students to learn the standard algorithms for addition, subtraction, multiplication and division.

In a recent letter to Dr. Nhung Tran-Davies, the campaigning mother who initiated the widely popular back-to-basics math petition, Dirks declined to meet with her and referred her to Amaya Ortigosa, Alberta Education's team leader for mathematics K–9. Considering that Ortigosa is a strong proponent of discovery learning, Tran-Davies is unlikely to get very far with her concerns.

To make matters worse, Dirks noted that even with the recent revisions, the math curriculum will not require students to learn the standard algorithms. Instead, it will continue to expect students to use a variety of problem-solving strategies, some more effective than others. In other words, nothing is going to change, and students and their parents can look forward to fuzzy math homework assignments for many years to come.

Unfortunately, there are other ways in which the Inspiring Education agenda is moving ahead. Alberta school boards are continuing with their plans to eliminate percentage grades from report cards and promote no-zero policies. The Calgary Board of Education (CBE), for example, recently removed percentage grades from all K–9 report cards and may soon do the same with report cards for grades 10–12.

Parents of K–9 students in Calgary must now wade through a series of checklists for various outcomes in each subject area in order to find out how their children are doing. With no percentage grades and only four achievement levels for each outcome, it will be difficult for parents to help their children set goals for improving their performance. More importantly, students will only receive two formal report cards each year. As a result, parents will get only one opportunity to review a formal report card and help their children before year-end.

On its website, the CBE notes that "Alberta is shifting toward a new vision for education based on the information gathered through Inspiring Education." Like many other school divisions in the province, the

CBE is still redesigning assessment and reporting practices to reflect this old policy direction. In other words, the CBE is acting as if there has not been a new mandate.

The CBE's commitment to fuzzy assessment policies goes even further. Its recommended reading list for parents includes, among other things, an article by Alfie Kohn, who says that schools should not give students any grades at all, and an article by Thomas Guskey, who says there are good reasons for no-zero policies. Obviously, the CBE would not recommend these articles to parents and teachers if they did not reflect the direction in which the board wishes to take its schools. All parents should be concerned about this direction.

Despite initial positive signs, Prentice and Dirks have yet to make meaningful changes to the misguided Inspiring Education initiative. Until they do, Alberta Education bureaucrats and school board officials will continue to dismantle this province's once top-performing education system. This does not bode well for students or their parents.

This article was originally published in 2014

~ 9 ~

THE OVERHYPED PROMISES OF TECHNOLOGY

STEVE JOBS AND Bill Gates are renowned for their technological inventions. As the founders of Apple and Microsoft, respectively, these two men did more to transform computers in the past half-century than virtually anyone else.

And yet, they both raised their kids in low-tech environments. Jobs refused to let his children play with the iPad he invented, while Gates didn't allow his children cell phones until they turned 14. Jobs and Gates were both worried about the negative impact technological devices could have on their children's development.

Unfortunately, many school leaders do not exercise the same level of caution. Instead, we hear about the need for schools to invest heavily in ICT. Technology proponents claim that schools need to teach digital literacy so students know how to use tech properly and responsibly.

This chapter provides a different perspective. Although technology can be a useful tool in classrooms, it should never be allowed to drive educational reform. The first article discusses an important study by the Kaiser Family Foundation that documents the dramatic increase in screen time among young people. The same study also found that students who were heavy media users were more likely than light media users to experience boredom, express dissatisfaction with school, indicate unhappiness with life, and get into trouble.

Other articles in the chapter challenge the way in which some schools are bringing electronic devices into the classroom without a proper implementation plan. This fixation on technology has led some educators to promote fads such as "flipped learning," where students do their homework during class time and watch instructional videos at home. One article identifies some major problems with the flipped learning approach.

With all the hype surrounding technology, it is easy to lose sight of traditional things that still matter in school. In light of this, one article defends the continued use of textbooks, while another argues that it is still important for students to learn cursive writing. The remaining articles describe some of the latest research on the impact of technological devices on learning and show that their use often does more harm than good.

Finally, the chapter concludes with an inspirational story about an elite private school in Australia that chose to severely restrict computer use among its younger students. The message of this chapter isn't that technology is bad, but rather that excessive use should be avoided. Ultimately, good teaching can take place with or without technology in the classroom.

TOO MUCH MEDIA IS A BAD MESSAGE

SMARTPHONES, IPADS, TEXTING, streaming, high-definition TV, e-books. All of these were virtually unheard of not so long ago and now they are commonplace. It shows just how quickly technology changes and the extent to which it dominates our lives.

In 2010, the Kaiser Family Foundation released a study entitled *Generation M2: Media in the Lives of 8- to 18-Year-Olds*. This survey of more than 2000 young people across the US found that their daily media usage had increased by more than 20% over the previous five years. In fact, young people spent more time using various forms of media than doing anything else, with the possible exception of sleeping.

Over that five-year period, the amount of time young people spent watching television rose by 16%, computer use increased by 44%, and time spent playing video games went up by a whopping 49%. Meanwhile, their time spent reading any form of print (i.e. books, newspapers, magazines) declined by almost 12%.

The study divided young people into three major categories: heavy users, moderate users, and light users. Heavy users were those who consumed more than 16 hours of media content in an average day, moderate users between three and 16 hours, while light users consumed fewer than three hours of media content. After controlling for variables such as age, race, and income-level, the researchers found that light media users had the highest levels of personal contentment in virtually every category measured, while heavy media users consistently had the lowest levels. Heavy media users were most likely to experience boredom, express dissatisfaction with school, indicate unhappiness with life, and get into trouble.

Something that should make all educators take note is the fact that heavy media users were more than twice as likely to receive poor grades in school as light media users. This provides a solid reason to question the argument that schools need to place greater emphasis on technology in the classroom.

It can be argued that schools have a role to play in educating students about the proper use of media, but an excessive focus on computer use at the early grade levels hardly seems the way to send this message. Schools should first and foremost focus on providing students with a solid grounding in the academic basics. Only once this is done should computers be introduced into the classroom – and, even then, in moderation.

A 2000 report produced by the Alliance for Childhood, *Fool's Gold: A Critical Look at Computers in Childhood*, backs up this recommendation by noting that there is no evidence that increased computer usage among younger students has a positive effect on academic achievement. The report also identifies the health hazards associated with sedentary habits and criticizes schools for promoting this lifestyle by overemphasizing the use of computers in the classroom.

Stanford University education professor Larry Cuban, former president of the American Educational Research Association, had this to say about technology in the classroom: " ... there is no clear, commanding body of evidence that students' sustained use of multimedia machines, the Internet, word processing, spreadsheets, and other popular applications has any impact on academic achievement."

However, what research does show is that students benefit greatly from face-to-face time with positive adult role models. So, instead of plopping a child in front of the television or allowing him to mindlessly surf the internet, parents would be well-advised to carefully guard against excessive use of technology.

Significantly, the Kaiser Family Foundation report found that parents who took measures to restrict the media usage of their children had a significant impact on the choices their children made. Proactive steps such as turning the television off during dinner, not putting televisions in bedrooms, and placing restrictions on computer access and video games substantially reduced the amount of media use by children.

Technology is here to stay, but parents and teachers need to do whatever they can to promote balanced usage. It does not make sense to allow young people to spend most of their waking hours watching television, texting, and surfing the internet. Let's all do our part to send the message that there is more to life than the latest piece of technology.

GADGETS IN CLASSROOMS ARE GIMMICKS

ACCORDING TO MANY education gurus, incorporating technology in the classroom is the key to a solid 21st-century education. As a result, school superintendents race to be the first to purchase the latest gadgets, while principals boast about the extent to which technology has been embedded in their schools.

In 2013, CBC Manitoba reported that a Winnipeg school division planned to make iPads mandatory in grades 6–8. During a public information session, parents were informed that tablet computers would soon become as essential in the classroom as basketballs were in a basketball game. The iPads were expected to replace textbooks, maps, and other printed classroom materials.

However, before rushing to equip schools with the latest technological gadgets, it would have been prudent to ask whether this would improve student learning. Considering the significant cost of purchasing, maintaining, and upgrading technological devices such as iPads, we need to ensure that it is not simply another expensive fad.

Peter Reimann and Anindito Aditomo of the University of Sydney have analyzed the research literature on the impact of technology on student achievement. Their findings were published in the *International Guide to Student Achievement* (2013). They concluded that most studies showed only a moderate academic benefit from technology and that "the effect of computer technology seems to be particularly small in studies that use either large samples or randomized control groups."

In other words, rigorous research studies reveal that the wholesale introduction of computer technology in classrooms has, at best, only a limited impact on student achievement. One needs to ask whether this modest benefit justifies making technology the focus of school reform.

Larry Cuban, a professor of education at Stanford University, certainly doesn't think so. In an article published in the April 17, 2013 edition of *Education Week*, Cuban notes that technology purveyors have claimed for decades that schools need the latest gadget to engage their students. He quotes an early typewriter ad that promises to "raise her marks," a filmstrip ad that says it can help "pupils comprehend faster," and an Apple ad that tells teachers an Apple IIe "makes it easy to become attached to your students." While the technology may change, the overblown promises remain the same.

If schools truly wish to improve academic achievement, they should focus on the three essentials of learning: a content-rich curriculum, sound lessons, and purposeful reading and writing in every discipline. In his book *Focus: Elevating the Essentials to Radically Improve Student Learning* (2011), Mike Schmoker demonstrates that schools focusing on these three things substantially outperform those that do not. According to Schmoker, technology is unnecessary when it comes to improving student achievement and too much emphasis on tech can get in the way of these learning essentials.

For example, Schmoker notes that reading properly written textbooks is the type of reading that students need to do more often. "Textbooks, along with other carefully selected nonfiction documents, afford students the kind of content-rich, semantically rich prose that . . . students need to acquire and critically process essential knowledge," he writes. While students may read some nonfiction on their iPads, it is unlikely they will read the same amount of dense, complex prose that they would normally encounter in a course textbook.

Some technology advocates suggest that iPads are better than regular textbooks because they can provide more up-to-date information to students. However, this argument overlooks the fact that most sound textbook content is not outdated. The history of Canadian Confederation remains the same now as it was ten years ago, as do most of the basic scientific concepts. When updates are needed, there is nothing stopping teachers from providing supplemental information to their students.

Anyone who thinks students will be left behind if schools do not incorporate the latest technological gadgets needs to take a deep breath. The reality is that students have no difficulty learning how to use technology, whether or not schools show them how to do it. In fact, using the latest technology is something that comes naturally to most young people. What does not come naturally is the kind of intense, systematic reading and writing that only happens if it is explicitly taught.

Before school administrators rush to adopt the latest technological gadget, they need to ask themselves whether it is the wisest course of action. Technology may be flashy and exciting, but it should not be the driver of education reform.

NEW TABLETS LESS USEFUL
THAN OLD MATH METHOD

MATH INSTRUCTION THIS fall is going to look quite different for approximately 300 Grade 7 students. Two major businesses and the province of Nova Scotia are providing the funds to purchase tablet computers for these students and their teachers. If this CA$1 million pilot project is successful, the program may be expanded to other grade levels and schools. I predict it will be a big success, but not because of the tablets.

Simply introducing more technology to classrooms has only a limited impact on learning and is hardly worth the significant costs involved. Instead, this pilot project will succeed because it will revolutionize math instruction. Why? Because these tablets will enable students to receive instruction from the Khan Academy, a non-profit education website created in 2006 by Salman Khan. With more than 3000 instructional videos available online at no charge, the Khan Academy is used by students around the world to learn about subjects as diverse as history, mathematics, and cosmology.

Anyone who takes the time to watch some of the instructional math videos on the Khan Academy website will see some familiar concepts. For example, the videos show how to add and subtract by placing one number on top of the other and working digit by digit from right to left. Multiplication is demonstrated using the standard vertical format, while the traditional long-division algorithm is consistently used as well.

In fact, all of the standard mathematical algorithms for addition, subtraction, multiplication, and division feature prominently in these videos. Interestingly, this is the exact opposite of the approach recommended by education faculties where teachers are trained.

Under the influence of math education professors, the standard algorithms have been systematically expunged from provincial curriculum guides and math textbooks. The underlying philosophy behind this "new math" approach is often called constructivism. Advocates say students need to construct their own ways of doing math. So, they argue, instead of showing students the most efficient way of solving a question, teachers should give them open-ended word problems and encourage them to invent their own problem-solving strategies.

One of the most prominent "new math" advocates was the late John Van de Walle, formerly a math education professor at Virginia Commonwealth University. In his widely circulated book series, *Teaching Student-Centered Mathematics*, Van de Walle disparaged the teaching of standard algorithms for addition, subtraction, multiplication, and division. He also argued that skill-based drill and practice made it harder for students to gain a deep conceptual understanding of mathematics.

Some math education professors go so far as to claim that teaching the standard algorithms to students is developmentally harmful. Constance Kamii, professor of early childhood education at the University of Alabama, co-authored a widely influential paper in 1998 entitled "The Harmful Effects of Algorithms in Grades 1–4." Even though the arguments contained in this paper have been thoroughly debunked by real math professors, Kamii's dubious research is regularly cited by "new math" advocates.

The Atlantic Canada Mathematics Curriculum, which is used in Nova Scotia, was strongly influenced by these education professors and their disciples. In addition, commonly used textbooks such as *Math Makes Sense* and *Math Focus* are heavily infused with the constructivist approach – it is almost impossible to find any standard algorithms in either of these textbook series. Instead, students are given convoluted word problems, poorly designed algorithms, and unclear directions.

So, when the Grade 7 students in this pilot project receive their tablets and watch the Khan Academy instructional videos featuring standard math algorithms, they will finally be exposed to math that makes sense. Once they learn the most efficient ways of solving math questions, they won't be particularly interested in going back to the fuzzy math that appears in their textbooks.

Of course, all of this could be done without bringing a single tablet into any classroom. Teachers could teach the standard algorithms using textbooks that actually contain proper step-by-step directions. Watching a solid instructional video about a math technique is good, but getting the same lesson from a classroom teacher who can answer questions is even better.

There is a certain amount of irony that the Nova Scotia students who use cutting-edge technology are going to end up learning math the old-fashioned way. The students in this pilot project are fortunate because they are going to do math properly, not because they get to play with tablets.

This article was originally published in 2013

TEXTBOOKS ARE
STILL IMPORTANT

THE LOWLY TEXTBOOK is under siege from progressive educators. Again.

Why waste money on textbooks, these educators argue, when all the information students ever need is available at the click of a mouse? Besides, they add, textbooks are hopelessly outdated and very biased.

These and other arguments were made in January 2014 by the history teacher David Cutler, writing in *The Atlantic* magazine. Predictably, Cutler claimed that over-reliance on textbooks early in his career resulted in apathy and boredom among his students. Things improved substantially when he moved away from textbooks and introduced a variety of other sources to his students.

Cutler also pointed to his experience as a graduate student. None of his history professors relied to any significant degree on textbooks. Rather, they provided relevant primary sources and realistic case studies that helped him to understand the information better than memorizing facts and dates from textbooks. Cutler argues that the same holds true for high school students.

These arguments may initially seem compelling, but they are actually fallacious. For example, it is misleading to compare high school students with graduate students. University students, particularly those at the graduate level, are highly motivated and come into their courses with substantial background knowledge in their discipline. Often these students can already recite hundreds of facts and dates by memory. As a result, there is little need to review basic timelines and key events. Rather, graduate students can dive right in to more advanced topics.

In contrast, most high school students know little about history. Consequently, a well-designed textbook is an invaluable tool. Not only does it serve as a useful reference guide, but it also presents key events in their proper chronological sequence and puts facts and dates into a broad historical context.

Shaping Canada by Linda Connor, Brian Hull, and Connie Wyatt-Anderson is an excellent Canadian example. As the recommended textbook for Manitoba's Grade 11 students, *Shaping Canada* provides a chronological overview of Canadian history and contains many excerpts from primary sources to give students a better understanding of life in the past.

History teachers can and should go beyond the information provided in textbooks, but it helps if they provide students with a book that contains most of the concepts and information they are expected to learn. Furthermore, high-quality textbooks such as *Shaping Canada* are extensively reviewed by subject matter experts and representatives from various ethnic groups, who together identify and weed out errors and misrepresentations. The result is a book that, while still imperfect, reflects more than one author's perspective.

As for the suggestion that widespread internet access makes textbooks obsolete, the reality is that the quality of online information varies widely. Websites are a hit-and-miss collection of good and bad sources, while a well-written textbook synthesizes the most important information in a way that students can easily understand.

Unless students already have substantial knowledge and considerable discernment, they are unlikely to find the same quality of information on the internet.

In addition, students need to be regularly challenged by their readings. As Mike Schmoker notes in his book *Focus: Elevating the Essentials to Radically Improve Student Learning* (2011), textbooks provide "the kind of content-rich, semantically rich prose that ... students need to acquire and critically process essential knowledge." So not only does reading the dense, challenging prose found in well-written textbooks impart content knowledge, but it also helps students to improve their reading skills.

Unfortunately, not all teachers are equally conversant with the subjects they teach. While it is desirable for all history courses to be taught by teachers with a strong history background, the reality is that some lack this expertise. For these teachers, textbooks are even more essential. It would be a shame to deprive them of this valuable tool.

That being said, although textbooks are undoubtedly useful, teachers should never rely on them exclusively. A good history teacher will, for example, use outside sources and ensure that students learn much more than what is written in their textbooks. Teachers should neither overly depend on textbooks nor be too quick to dismiss them.

Despite the substantial attacks on textbooks by progressive educators, it is far too soon to consign them to the dustbin of history.

HANDWRITING IS
A TIMELESS SKILL

MANY PROGRESSIVE EDUCATORS believe that handwriting is obsolete in the 21st century. It isn't hard to see how they came to this conclusion. Computers are everywhere and an increasing number of schools expect students, even those in Grade 1, to do their work on tablets. So why bother teaching students how to handwrite?

Unfortunately, much of the debate about handwriting tends to dwell on minor issues. For example, supporters and opponents of handwriting argue about how often students will find themselves in situations where computers are not available. They squabble over whether handwritten signatures on legal documents will eventually be replaced by electronic signatures. Finally, they differ on the need for students to read historical documents in their original, handwritten form.

However, as important as these questions seem, they miss the bigger picture. The more important issue is whether learning how to handwrite helps students to master important skills such as reading, and whether writing words on paper is better for learning than typing them on tablets. If the answer to these questions is yes, then it makes sense to keep paper and pencils in the classroom.

Fortunately, research gives us a clear answer. Dr. Hetty Roessingh is a professor in the Werklund School of Education at the University of Calgary and an expert in the field of language and literacy. She has found that making students print letters by hand, particularly before the end of Grade 2, plays an important role in their reading development.

According to Roessingh, printing creates memory traces in the brain that assist with the recognition of letter shapes. Typing on a keyboard does not have the same impact. In other words, handwriting helps students to move information from their short-term memories into their long-term memories, while typing does not.

When students practice printing by hand, they learn how to read and write more quickly and more accurately. Contrary to popular myth, repetition is not a bad thing. Only by committing foundational skills to long-term memory can students move on to more advanced tasks. Students who get insufficient practice in printing letters by hand invariably develop weaker writing skills than students who regularly practice the skill.

In the upper elementary grades, it is still important for students to learn cursive writing. Roessingh notes that connecting letters together in a script makes it possible for students to write more quickly and this contributes to the quality of the writing outcomes. "When writing by hand becomes both legible and fluent, reflecting a sense of automaticity, the writer is able to generate more text. Precious, scarce working memory spaces become available to select better vocabulary and get it into the page in interesting, organized ways," explains Roessingh.

The importance of automaticity is strongly supported by cognitive psychologists. As Drs. Jeroen van Merriënboer and John Sweller note in the June 2005 edition of *Educational Psychology Review*, our working memory has a very limited storage capacity. In order to make proper use of it, we need to transfer information to our long-term memory. We then organize this information into various "cognitive schemata" that help us to solve more complex problems. Thus, students who handwrite fluently can engage with more challenging text than students who still struggle with basic vocabulary, because more information has been transferred to their long-term memories.

Learning does not come automatically. For most students it is genuinely hard work, as our brains are not naturally wired for the foundational skills of reading and writing. To achieve mastery, these skills need to be explicitly taught, regularly practiced, and constantly reinforced. Learning how to write individual letters and words by hand, and doing so fluently, is essential to entrench reading as an automatic skill.

In contrast, primary-grade students who do their assignments on keyboards and tablets miss out on this valuable skill development. Instead of training their brains to memorize particular letters each time they painstakingly print a word, they simply press a button to get the letter they want. Often the spell-check feature supplies the correct spellings, so students never learn how to independently spell more challenging words.

Far from being obsolete, handwriting will remain an important skill in the 21st century and beyond. Paper and pencil may not be as flashy as the latest tablet, but they do help students to learn a lot more. Sometimes the simple things really do work best.

TECHNOLOGY SHOULD NOT
DRIVE EDUCATION REFORM

A 2015 REPORT from the Organisation for Economic Co-operation and Development (OECD) came as a bombshell to those who view technology as the driving force of education reform. The report found that "students who use computers very frequently at school do a lot worse in most learning outcomes, even after accounting for social background and student demographics."

Not only is this mindset incredibly expensive, but it also often undermines student learning. At the same time, it is important not to react too far in the opposite direction. The report's author, OECD education director Andreas Schleicher, does not advocate removing all computers from schools – they do have some benefits. For example, computers make it possible for teachers to provide up-to-date information to students, particularly in subjects like science where new discoveries happen regularly. Banishing computers from classrooms, particularly in high school, would be an unfortunate overreaction to Schleicher's report.

So why does technology have such a poor track record in improving student achievement? After all, the OECD report is not nearly the first time education researchers have pointed out the limited benefits of technology in schools. Larry Cuban, an education professor at Stanford University, has said for years that technology manufacturers regularly make overblown and unsubstantiated promises about the latest gadgets.

Even researchers who believe that technology is beneficial in classrooms have warned against implementing it uncritically. In the *International Guide to Student Achievement* (2013), Peter Reimann and Anindito Aditomo of the University of Sydney review a number of research studies and find that technology has "a positive, albeit small, impact on students' achievement across many content areas." They go on to caution that "claims that any particular technology will necessarily bring large, radical, or revolutionary improvement in academic achievement should be met with skepticism."

Perhaps the best way to address this issue is to ask what actually has the biggest impact on student achievement. The answers are not hard to find. Strong teacher-student relationships, direct instruction, coherent curricula, focused practice, and timely feedback from teachers all have large positive impacts on student achievement. Each of these can take place in the presence or absence of technology. So, neither implementing nor removing technology is the key to improving student achievement.

Unfortunately, some of the strongest advocates of integrating technology in the classroom are simultaneously pushing education reforms that go against the research evidence. One of the most obvious examples is Alberta's Inspiring Education initiative, which downplays the need for teachers to impart specific knowledge and skills to students. Nowhere is this blind adherence to ideology more apparent than in the province's stubborn refusal to abandon discovery math, despite mountains of research showing the superiority of direct instruction and focused practice.

The age-old saying that a teacher should be a guide on the side rather than a sage on the stage is not only bad poetry, it is also bad advice. Teachers *should* be front and centre in the classroom. They should be teaching, explaining new concepts, showing students how to solve problems, and providing immediate, corrective feedback so students can fix their mistakes right away and not two weeks later. Teachers should be encouraged to set the direction of learning and provide clear, focused lessons.

All too often, technology is used to push teachers off to the side and de-emphasize direct instruction. It is no coincidence that the wholesale adoption of technology in the classroom is a central component of Inspiring Education. In fact, the Inspiring Education blueprint goes so far as to say that students need to "use these new technologies as designers and creators of knowledge." In other words, teachers should just get out of the way and let students get on with the business of creating new knowledge – a surefire recipe for educational failure.

When technology leads to a greater reliance on ineffective instructional practices, it is bound to have a negative impact on student achievement. The OECD report serves as a poignant reminder that it is a mistake to put all your educational eggs in the technology basket. Instead, schools should focus on doing the things actually supported by the evidence. The quality of teaching is far more important than the type of technology used in the classroom.

STEPPING BACK FROM THE COMPUTER CRAZE

ONE OF AUSTRALIA'S largest and most prestigious private schools certainly went against the grain last week. Sydney Grammar School no longer allows students to bring laptops to school and requires all assignments to be handwritten until students begin high school. This stands in sharp contrast to the widespread and enthusiastic adoption of technology in many other schools.

Sydney Grammar School's headmaster, John Vallance, did not mince words when interviewed by *The Australian* newspaper. He described the billions of dollars spent on computers in schools as "a scandalous waste of money" and added that "this investment in classroom technology is going to be seen as a huge fraud."

Lest anyone dismiss Vallance as a cantankerous technophobe, it should be noted that he has a distinguished academic background, including a doctorate from Cambridge University. He has served as headmaster at Sydney Grammar School for 18 years and was appointed by the Australian government in 2014 as a specialist reviewer of the national arts curriculum. So, when it comes to curriculum and instruction, Vallance knows what he is talking about.

Furthermore, Sydney Grammar School is one of the top-performing schools in Australia and counts among its alumni many prominent business leaders and at least three former prime ministers. At more than AU$32,000 per year, tuition is extremely steep. Parents aren't going to pay that amount of money if they don't see some impressive results.

Vallance can also point to significant research that backs up his concerns about the overuse of technology in schools. For example, a major report released last year by the Organisation for Economic Co-operation and Development (OECD) found that technology had only a mixed impact on student achievement. "In fact, PISA

[Programme for International Student Assessment] results show no appreciable improvements in student achievement in reading, mathematics, or science in the countries that had invested heavily in ICT for education," the report stated.

However, while Vallance is right to be concerned about the overuse of technology in schools, removing computers entirely from classrooms might be a step too far. For example, the OECD report also found that moderate access to technology in school had a positive impact on academic achievement. So, although excessive computer use can harm student achievement, moderate access is often helpful.

In the *International Guide to Student Achievement* (2013), Peter Reimann and Anindito Aditomo of the University of Sydney reviewed the research and found that, most of the time, "ICT does have a positive, albeit relatively small, impact on students' achievement across many content areas." At the same time, Reimann and Aditomo cautioned that "claims that any particular technology, in and of itself, will bring large, radical, or revolutionary impact on achievement should be meet with skepticism."

In light of these findings, it is appropriate to be skeptical about the overhyped promises made by technology proponents. Contrary to what some advocates claim, textbooks and other written materials are far from obsolete. Students are more likely to engage with densely written prose when reading quality textbooks than when surfing the internet. Simply put, traditional hardcover and paperback books are here for the long haul and won't disappear anytime soon.

When it comes to ICT in schools, a balanced approach is needed. Technology must never be allowed to become the driving force of instructional reform. Research is clear that the quality of teaching has a much larger impact on student achievement than the amount of technology in classrooms. Good teaching can and does take place in both the presence and absence of technology.

This article was originally published in 2016

COMMON SENSE

« 10 »

THE MERITS
OF SCHOOL
CHOICE

PICTURE A SCHOOL in an underprivileged part of north London, England. One-third of nearby families live in poverty, a significant percentage are visible minorities, and the neighbourhood crime rate is twice the national average. What type of results would you expect students at this school to get on their General Certificate of Secondary Education (GCSE) exams?

If you assumed that they would score significantly below the national average, your thinking is consistent with those who argue that a school's neighbourhood has a much more important impact on student achievement than the quality of instruction within the school. This defeatist mentality is common in progressive education circles.

However, the school in question is Michaela Community School, one of the top-performing schools in the UK. In fact, Michaela's students scored four times higher than the national average on their GCSE exams. Michaela takes a traditional approach, with a strong focus on content knowledge and lots of practice and memorization. Discipline is strict and teachers are expected to be in control of the students in their classrooms. All students are held to high academic and behavioural standards regardless of their home lives.

Michaela Community School has one other important characteristic. It is a free school (the approximate equivalent of charter schools in Canada and the US) and operates independently of the state-controlled system. Like other free schools, Michaela does not charge tuition fees to students, is state-funded, and must abide by the same admissions code as other public schools. As long as free schools follow basic government standards, they are free to offer educational programs as they see fit.

Progressive educators typically oppose any form of school choice. Even when Michaela Community School posted impressive GCSE results, some critics continued to attack the school's traditional approach as being harmful to students. However, school choice is not about undermining the public school system, but about improving the performance of students and increasing the educational options available to parents. Considering the huge demand for traditional education, free schools provide an alternative that might otherwise not be available in public education systems in Britain, Canada, or the US.

This chapter focuses on school choice within the Canadian context, where there is, in fact, little choice. The first article explains the unique approach of Edmonton

Public Schools, a school board that embraces choice. Within the Edmonton public system, one can find traditional schools, progressive schools, sports-focused schools, and even religious schools. There is considerably less demand for private schools in Edmonton because the public system is flexible enough to accommodate the wide needs of parents and children for particular forms of education.

Other articles describe the charter school system in Alberta. In particular, Foundations for the Future Charter Academy in Calgary shares many similarities with Michaela Community School, in that it has a traditional approach to education. Foundations for the Future is so popular with parents that there are currently thousands of students on the waiting list.

Another issue that is addressed is public funding going to private schools. Instead of saying that this wastes money by shifting it from one system to another, it is more accurate to say that money follows the student. In other words, the state invests in students, not in schools. As long as a school meets provincial curriculum standards and hires qualified teachers, it makes sense for government money to follow students to whichever school they choose to attend.

School choice is not a panacea, but it makes options available to parents and children that might otherwise be out of their reach. It also makes it possible for schools to break free from the government monopoly and offer alternative approaches to education.

SCHOOL BOARDS COULD
START A REVOLUTION

LIKE MANY OTHER urban school divisions, the Toronto District School Board continues to struggle with declining enrolment due to private school competition and parents who move to the suburbs. But a plan for the development of specialty schools could be just the thing needed to rejuvenate Toronto's stagnating public school system – provided it does it right.

According to the education director, the Toronto board plans to allow four specialized elementary schools to open in September 2011: a school for boys, a school for girls, a choir school, and a sports academy. They will operate within the public system and have an open enrolment policy. No tuition fees will be charged.

Allowing parents more choice is a welcome change from the usual one-size-fits-all model imposed on neighbourhoods by public school boards. By enabling the creation of specialty schools within the public system, the boards can meet the needs of parents who would otherwise choose to enrol their children in private schools.

What's happening in Toronto is by no means unique. More than two decades ago, the Edmonton Public School Board launched a revolutionary set of changes when it made choice the foundation of its approach to education. Edmonton has specialty schools that focus on Aboriginal education, sports, science, the Waldorf approach, Christian education, and performing arts. Parents also have the option of regular neighbourhood schools.

In many cities there has been an exodus of students from public schools, but Edmonton has experienced the reverse. Because of the many choices available to parents within the public system, there is little need for private school options. In fact, some of Edmonton's public schools are former private schools that joined the public system because of the flexibility provided by the board.

For this success to be replicated in other cities, such as Toronto, there are a number of issues that school boards need to keep in mind. First, the boards must embrace choice as an integral part of their overall philosophy, not simply as another fad to implement on a trial basis in a few isolated pockets. It is positive that Toronto will allow for several specialty schools, but the board should go much further. There is no reason to limit choice to only a few groups of parents. All parents should be able to pick the school that best meets the needs of their children.

Second, it's important to allow a variety of specialty schools to emerge. As long as schools follow the basic curriculum and all other provincial guidelines, there is no reason for boards to arbitrarily restrict specialty schools to those preferred by individual board members or administrators. Limited choice results in limited results. If the numbers warrant it, parents should be able to have a school that emphasizes the specialty of their choice.

Another key aspect of the Edmonton model is how principals are given control over their own budgets – this allows them to create the most effective environment possible. More than 90% of every dollar raised by the Edmonton Public School Board is controlled at the . local level by individual principals. This flexibility gives them the authority they need to manage their schools effectively.

But local school autonomy needs to be combined with accountability. Edmonton principals are held accountable for their results: students write regular standards tests in the core academic subjects, with each school's results made available to the public. As a result, this information becomes part of what parents take into account when deciding where to enrol their children.

In short, school boards need to ensure that choice is made available to all parents. They need to be open to a variety of specialty options, give principals greater autonomy, and hold schools accountable for their results through the use of standardized achievement tests in the core subjects.

If Toronto and other urban school boards follow Edmonton's lead, Canadians could witness a revolution in the quality of education provided to our children.

This article was originally published in 2010

MONEY SHOULD
FOLLOW THE STUDENT

THE SASKATCHEWAN GOVERNMENT'S recent decision to extend provincial funding to independent schools brings the province in line with the three other Western provinces. Saskatchewan independent schools are now eligible for funding equivalent to 50% of the provincial per-student average, provided they follow the provincial curriculum and hire certified teachers.

An editorial in *The Globe and Mail* criticizing this decision argued that funding independent schools emphasized separateness rather than diversity. It raised the spectre of John Tory's disastrous 2007 election campaign pledge to fund independent Ontario schools, and ominously warned that the general public was worried about any policies that appeared to promote segregation.

However, such criticisms overlook the fact that some level of funding for independent schools is already well-established in Canada. Ontario, Saskatchewan, and Alberta provide 100% funding to their separate (Roman Catholic) school boards. These arrangements are entrenched in our Constitution. Combine this with the partial funding available to independent schools in British Columbia, Alberta, and Manitoba, and it is obvious that some provinces do not limit their education funding to public schools alone.

Opposition to provincial funding for independent schools tends to be based on three key points. The first is that many independent schools are faith-based and governments have no business funding religious organizations. The second focuses on the role played by public schools in integrating their students into mainstream society, and how independent schools promote segregation instead. Finally, opponents argue that since students from wealthy families are most likely to attend private schools, the policy amounts to a subsidy for the rich.

These arguments seem convincing because the current arrangements for public, separate, and independent schools focus on funding school boards and/or individual schools. This shifts debate toward which school system is most worthy of public funding.

Adopting a model in which the money follows the student would be a better way to handle the question. It would move us away from the tiresome debate about funding independent schools and put the emphasis on the choices made by students and their parents. Under this model, each student would attend the school of his or her choice. A school's provincial funding would thus depend on the number of students enrolled, provided it followed the provincial curriculum and demonstrated that students were learning it.

Any school that chooses to follow the provincial curriculum and receives the full public funding allocated for each student can be considered a public school, regardless of its philosophical or religious orientation. Although it is important to hold all schools accountable for their academic results, it makes little sense to assume that a one-size-fits-all approach is suitable for Canada's diverse population. Students should choose the school that best meets their needs. Providing flexibility at the local level is important to ensuring this happens.

As for the concern about subsidizing private schooling for wealthy families, a policy of funding the student actually equalizes educational opportunities for families with limited means. It makes them the primary beneficiaries, because it enables them to choose schooling options currently beyond their reach due to financial limitations.

Every province should provide funding that follows students to whatever accredited school they attend, whether classified as public, separate, or independent.

Letting the money follow the student is an important component of ensuring everyone gets the best education possible. Although Saskatchewan's funding decision does not get there, it brings students in the province closer to the option for greater choice.

This article was originally published in 2012

CHARTING A NEW COURSE
FOR SMALL SCHOOLS

THE PAST FEW years have been difficult ones for public education in Nova Scotia. Declining student enrolment, poor academic results, and unpopular school closures are just a few of the problems facing this province.

When it comes to school closures, trustees and parents are caught in a vicious cycle. As student numbers decline, the province reduces funding to public school boards. In order to balance their budgets, boards make unpopular decisions to close schools. Parents feel powerless as trustees ignore their impassioned pleas to keep community schools open.

However, instead of making parents fight a hopeless battle against monolithic and unresponsive school boards, Nova Scotia should give them the tools they need to take meaningful action. It should follow the example of Alberta and pass charter schools legislation.

Charter schools are public schools that operate independently of school boards. They are governed by non-profit organizations and receive an annual per-student operational grant from the province. Charter schools have no religious affiliation, practice an open enrolment policy, and follow the provincial curriculum. Currently, 13 charter schools operate in Alberta.

Parents in rural Nova Scotia should take note of recent events in the tiny hamlet of Valhalla Centre in northwest Alberta. Several years ago, Valhalla Centre nearly lost its community school. However, instead of allowing the school board to proceed with closure, parents and other community members banded together, purchased the building from the board, and established Valhalla Community School as an independently operated charter school.

Because the school now operates independently of the board, the community has adopted a charter that reflects local concerns and values. Valhalla Community School places a strong emphasis on rural leadership, and requires its students to learn about board governance and parliamentary procedure. It also focuses on teacher-directed instruction, classical literature, drill and practice in mathematics, and accurate spelling and grammar. Interestingly, since becoming a charter school, enrolment has grown steadily as it attracts students from the wider geographical area.

Imagine what Nova Scotia parents could do if they had the same opportunity to establish charter schools as parents in Alberta. Charter schools legislation would make it possible for parents to keep their schools open and refashion them to better reflect the values of the local community.

Not only that, but charter schools can also revolutionize education in urban centres. Consider the example of Foundations for the Future Charter Academy (FFCA) in Calgary, Alberta. FFCA was established almost 20 years ago and its enrolment has grown to almost 3000 students on seven campuses. Like Valhalla, FFCA places a strong emphasis on traditional academics and hard work. FFCA students wear uniforms, complete regular homework, memorize their math facts, and learn to read by phonics. Its program is so popular with parents that it has 6000 students on its waiting list.

Many parents in Halifax, Nova Scotia, would be very interested if a school like FFCA opened in their city. Since charter schools do not charge tuition fees, admission would be open to all parents, not just those who can afford to pay. Parents dissatisfied with the instruction provided in regular public schools would finally have an alternative.

However, the range of potential charter schools goes far beyond those who prefer a traditional model of education. For example, the Boyle Street Education Centre in Calgary caters to at-risk youth in the 14–19 age group, while Mother Earth's Children's Charter School in Stony Plain focuses on Aboriginal education. In addition, the Suzuki Charter School in Edmonton promotes advanced music skills at an early age using the approach of the renowned musician Shinichi Suzuki. Clearly, charter schools reflect the diversity of Canadian society.

In contrast, the one-size-fits-all model of public education in Nova Scotia does not meet the needs of a diverse population. The natural trend towards increased central control by school board officials means principals have limited control over their own schools and simply follow the dictates of the board. Not only that, but recent controversies around school closures have also shown that school boards cannot effectively respond to the needs of parents and communities in the face of budget cuts.

Charter schools have the potential to transform public education in Nova Scotia. All the government needs to do is give them a chance.

This article was originally published in 2013

STUDENTS SHOULDN'T HAVE TO WAIT FOR A GOOD EDUCATION

PEOPLE SAY THAT good things come to those who wait. Maybe they do. But this saying is cold comfort to the families of more than 8000 children who are waiting to get into the most popular charter school in Calgary, Alberta.

Foundations for the Future Charter Academy (FFCA) has about 3000 students in its seven campuses across the city. The school would like to accept more students, but the Alberta government caps its enrolment. Meanwhile, families on the waiting list are left to wonder whether their kids will ever have the opportunity to attend.

It isn't hard to see why FFCA is so popular. Whereas regular public school administrators and school boards are largely under the sway of the latest edu-babble fads and failed progressive ideologies, FFCA encourages its teachers to use strategies that actually work. Among other things, this means teachers take charge of their classrooms and provide lots of teacher-directed instruction. In math class, students memorize their times tables, learn the standard algorithms for basic operations, and do lots of practice questions. In reading,

FFCA teachers make regular use of phonics because of its proven effectiveness. Students learn proper grammar, receive regular homework assignments, and write a lot of tests. Obviously, parents want their children to be able to calculate and read effectively.

These traditional methodologies are popular among parents and many teachers, yet they are anathema in education faculties where teachers are trained. Education professors regularly encourage prospective teachers to be a guide on the side rather than a sage on the stage. In other words, the last thing they want is for teachers to provide a defined knowledge base and skill set to students. They downplay the importance of academic content, instead focusing on social issues and student self-esteem.

The influence of this failed ideology can be found throughout the public school system. Fuzzy math, invented spelling, no-zero policies, incomprehensible report cards, and lax discipline are only a few examples. Parents are fed up with how their neighbourhood public schools have been turned into laboratories for a never-ending succession of senseless fads. They want their children to receive a solid education and consequently they flock to schools like FFCA.

At first glance, it seems surprising that such schools are not popping up across Canada. Considering the demand for a back-to-basics approach to education, there would be no shortage of students.

Unfortunately, despite all the lip service given to diversity, most public school boards are highly monolithic. With the notable exception of Edmonton Public Schools, the boards tend to control everything from teacher professional development to the textbooks used in class, leaving principals to simply implement board directives. Also, boards don't like it when students try to attend schools outside their designated catchment areas, throwing up as many roadblocks as possible. It's not surprising that principals usually fall in line.

If it wasn't for the Alberta charter school legislation, passed in 1994, FFCA wouldn't exist today. Charter schools are public schools that operate outside the jurisdiction of public school boards. Like other public schools, they are non-sectarian, open to all students, and do not charge fees. However, their autonomy makes it possible for them to offer courses and programs, such as basic math and English, which simply do not exist in public school boards. Hence, FFCA's back-to-basics approach is serving the needs of students.

While charter schools are common in the US, Alberta is the only Canadian province that allows them to exist. As a result, FFCA won't be opening up sister branches in other parts of the country, no matter how much demand there is. Even in Alberta, charter schools don't exactly have it easy. The government allows only 15 to exist at a time and makes each one reapply for a charter every five years. The government also caps enrolment at each school so it cannot expand to take in more students.

Charter schools like FFCA have proven their worth to students and parents. If Alberta made it easier for new ones to exist and provided more support to those that do, fewer students would need to sit on a waiting list. As for the rest of the country, it's time to follow Alberta's example and give charter schools a chance to revolutionize public education.

FURTHER READING

LIKE ALL WRITERS, I stand on the shoulders of giants. These excellent books have significantly influenced my thinking on education and my teaching practice. For teachers, parents, and other concerned citizens who are interested in exploring educational issues further, these books are a great place to start.

Ashman, Greg. *The Truth About Teaching: An Evidence-Informed Guide for New Teachers*. London: SAGE Publications, Ltd, 2018

Bennett, Tom. *Teacher Proof: Why Research in Education Doesn't Always Mean What It Claims, and What You Can Do About It*. New York: Routledge, 2013

Carey, Benedict. *How We Learn: The Surprising Truth About When, Where, and Why It Happens*. New York: Random House, 2016

Chall, Jeanne. *The Academic Achievement Challenge: What Really Works in the Classroom?* New York: Guilford Press, 2000

Christodoulou, Daisy. *Seven Myths About Education*. New York: Routledge, 2014

Hattie, John, and Anderman, Eric M. (eds). *International Guide to Student Achievement*. New York: Routledge, 2013

Hattie, John, and Yates, Gregory. *Visible Learning and the Science of How We Learn*. New York: Routledge, 2014

Hattie, John. *Visible Learning: A Synthesis of Over 800 Meta-Analyses Relating to Achievement*. New York: Routledge, 2009

Hirsch, Jr., E. D. *The Knowledge Deficit: Closing the Shocking Education Gap for American Children*. Boston: Houghton-Mifflin Company, 2006

Hirsch, Jr., E. D. *The Schools We Need and Why We Don't Have Them*. New York: Random House, 1996

Hirsch, Jr., E. D. *Why Knowledge Matters: Rescuing Our Children From Failed Educational Theories.* Cambridge: Harvard Education Press, 2016

Holmes, Mark. *The Reformation of Canada's Schools: Breaking the Barriers to Parental Choice.* Montreal: McGill-Queen's University Press, 1998

Lapointe, Marc. *Standing in the Education Gap: A Commonsense Approach to Helping Your Child Succeed in School.* Bloomington: iUniverse, 2013

Nichols, Tom. *The Death of Expertise: The Campaign Against Established Knowledge and Why It Matters.* New York: Oxford University Press, 2017

Nikiforuk, Andrew. *School's Out: The Catastrophe in Public Education and What We Can Do About It.* Toronto: Macfarlane Walter & Ross, 1993

Ravitch, Diane. *Left Back: A Century of Failed School Reforms.* New York: Simon & Schuster, 2000

Schmoker, Mike. *Focus: Elevating the Essentials to Radically Improve Student Learning.* Alexandria: ASCD, 2011

Sherrington, Tom. *The Learning Rainforest: Great Teaching in Real Classrooms.* Melton: John Catt Educational Ltd, 2017

Wexler, Natalie. *The Knowledge Gap: The Hidden Cause of America's Broken Education System – and How to Fix It.* New York: Penguin Random House, 2019

Willingham, Daniel T. *When Can You Trust the Experts? How to Tell Good Science From Bad in Education.* San Francisco: Jossey-Bass, 2012

Willingham, Daniel T. *Why Don't Students Like School? A Cognitive Scientist Answers Questions About How the Mind Works and What It Means for the Classroom.* San Francisco: Jossey-Bass, 2009

.